FROM THIS
FERTILE VALLEY

Martha Lou Perritti

MARTHA LOU PERRITTI

FROM THIS FERTILE VALLEY

The Life of a Military Wife

ISBN: 978-1-58320-038-4
Printed in the United States by Lifestyles Press

For my Husband
Frank Victor Perritti, Jr.

Tribute to my Friend
Judith M. McLeran

Also by Martha Lou Perritti

Crossing in the Rain

Standing Against the Wind

Cooking Our Way

Martha Lou's Kitchen

CONTENTS

Part I

Part II

Part III

PREFACE

Jumping off the old wooden porch, I managed to land both bare feet firmly into the Alabama red dirt. As I maintained my balance, I felt what seemed to be a pebble stuck to the bottom of one of my feet. Shaking my foot loosened the object and it fell to the ground. It was my lucky day. I had found a penny!

Old man Cantrel's country grocery store, not even the size of our present day convenient stores, stood about forty feet from the edge of the two-lane Trinity Highway. The weather-beaten siding had at one time been white-washed and the Coca Cola and Merita bread signs were hardly visible. The wooden porch extended about eight feet from the screen door and was wide enough for a rocking chair.

Picking up the penny, I turned to see Old Man Cantrel watching me.

"Here Mister Cantrel," I said, reaching to hand him the penny, "this belongs to you. Someone must have dropped it before they could pay for their groceries."

I will never forget what the old man said to me. "No, my child, someone dropped it while leaving my store and had already paid me. I don't know who that person was, so the penny belongs to you. You found it."

Clenching the penny in my fist, I protected it until I got home where I placed it in my little secret box I kept under the bed that I slept in with two of my sisters. I would show it to Daddy when he comes home.

All of my life, to me, there has been something special about finding a penny on the ground. Who does it belong to? Where has it been? Is it now mine to keep? Daddy explained to me that finding a penny meant good luck would come. He said, "It's your lucky day!"

On that day in front of Old Man Cantrel's store I was only four years old. Although it has been 63 years since I found that first penny, my fascination with finding pennies has never changed.

In order to understand why pennies are so important to me, you have to know the story of my life. There seem to have been three different beginnings and endings of my life from 1939 until 2007.

I was born in my grandmother's house that stood in the middle of a cotton field in the valley of the Tennessee River of North Alabama. My mother had eight babies before me and one after. During the early years of my life, Mother kept her children on the farm in the valley. In order to put food on the table, she grew a vegetable garden, corn and sugar cane crops. Share cropping cotton fields was done for money to buy clothes and other things. Dad was gone from home most of the time, working in Birmingham as a house painter.

We had very little money, very little of anything, so you see saving lost pennies could buy me a candy bar or peppermint stick.

I lived at home with my parents until I was 23 years old. In 1962, I became a military wife and until 1977 that defined my life.

After my husband retired from the military in 1977, we lived for several years near Orlando, Florida. During those years, my son graduated from college and joined the United States Air Force. Frank, my husband, owned a landscaping business and I took a job as credit manager/ office manager of Jacobson's Department Store.

1990 brought about a lifestyle change for us. We moved to Pine Island, Florida. This was the perfect place for retirement years and to grow old; but, before the growing old thing, I had something I needed to do. I was ready to make my dream of writing a book come true.

I did just that. I published **Crossing in the Rain; Standing Against the Wind, Cooking Our Way** and **Martha Lou's Kitchen.**

I was fifty years old when the third part of my life began. Now I live the life of an author/lecturer. This book, **From This Fertile Valley**, is my historical novel trilogy.

All the years of my life I followed the path of my dream. How many pennies have I found along that path? I wish I had saved them.

PROLOGUE

I have shared my family history on the pages of two books, **Standing Against the Wind** and **Crossing In the Rain**. People who have read these books ask me, "Are you going to write a book about your life?" I have resisted the idea because I don't want to be portrayed as being an egotistical author. My decision to write a book about my life comes with the hope it will be seen as an extension of my heritage. As I document the facts of my life, I express my gratitude to my ancestors: my Cherokee mothers and my Irish fathers.

The character of my life was determined long before I began to live it. The Cherokee Indian and the Irish were people accustomed to difficulty challenges, hard work and positive results. My life has been a summation of these attributes. Benefiting from the inner strength of my ancestors, I followed my own path. I take pride in my accomplishments, my friends and my family. Continuing my journey, I leave behind my written trilogy and always hope for a better tomorrow.

FROM THIS FERTILE VALLEY

PART
I

"Trail out of the Warrior Mountains"

Chapter 1

Descending the Warrior Mountains

Soaring through the winds of the forest, the eagle spans his wings, his call echoing in the Warrior Mountains. Lingering at the end of the porch, Rebekah reached to touch her rose bush. It was bare from season's growth, no blooms, few leaves, so she left it there.

A foggy mist hung low, like a shroud, over the Cheatem Trail. Pulling the wagon ever so slowly, the two mules hung heir heads as though they sensed the sorrow of the family. Grandpa James gripped the reins trying to avoid the spotty mud holes in the narrow road. "Easy boys, easy," he uttered almost in a whisper.

Seated next to Grandpa on the wagon seat, Grandma Lucinda wrapped her woolen shawl around her shoulders. She didn't look back, no words spoken and no tears. Descending the mountain, there was no laughter from the children.

They had lived under the canopy of the forest. Now they must leave. Their home place would be weathered in time.

My mother, Rebekah, sat in the back of the wagon. Ninety-eight years had passed since a young Cherokee Indian girl had ridden in a wagon leaving the Cumberland Gap. Great, great, great, Grandma Polly was five years old when she began her journey. Mother, Rebekah, was fourteen. They both faced an uncertain future. Once the U.S. government began moving the Cherokee from their land, there was no turning back. What began in the early 1800s continued into the 1900s. The government, under the presidency of William Taft, had delayed implementing the enforcement of forestland taking. However, after President Woodrow Wilson took office in 1913, the National Forest Commission established the Alabama Purchase Unit in 1914. Plans that had begun in the early 1900s were now put into effect. The people who lived in the forest of the Warrior Mountains, North Alabama, must now move out. This was to be accomplished by whatever means necessary.

1916, the men in black suits stood on Grandpa's porch. The deal was made: one dollar and fifty cents an acre for one hundred sixty-five acres of land. Just as great, great, great grandmother Polly and the Cherokee people had survived the American Revolution, the Trail of Tears, and the Civil War, these members of my family were forced from their land in the Alabama forest.

In the distance stood the Warrior Mountains, their homeland. As this distance grew, Grandpa James tried to suppress his anger over the dramatic change in his life.

"We will have to continue to live our lives as best we can," consoled Grandma Lucinda. She possessed the strength and courage of her Cherokee ancestors. The passage of time had not changed the options for my family. They must learn to live a new way of life.

If changes were to be made, their children must make them. Out of the Cumberland Gap had come a young Indian girl named Polly; now, generations later, five young girls were leaving the forest to face the challenge of their future.

As the generations of a family weave the fabric of a nation, they were plagued with the stigma of Indian blood. Their need for acceptance in a society outside the forest caused descendants to outwardly deny their heritage.

The oldest of the five girls, Rebekah, had experienced the cruelty of children's prejudice in school. At an early age, she realized that if she had children of her own, she must protect them so they could accomplish their goals in the white man's world.

Leaving their past in the forest, denying their heritage, it would take many families one hundred years before they returned to their roots.

I was sixty years old when I learned of my Cherokee heritage. I am not sure if having known this would have changed my life in any way. I do know that now it is a wonderful feeling to be able to examine and understand the people and from where I came.

I grew up knowing my mother's strengths and now I share the memories of her with the spirits of my ancestors.

"Fertile Fields of the Tennessee Valley."

Chapter 2

The Tennessee Valley

Following the Cheatem Trail northward out of the Warrior Mountains, my ancestors entered what has come to be known as the "Tennessee Valley."

Perhaps as early as 8,000 B.C. the gradual warming of the earth's atmosphere caused the end of what we call the Ice Age.

In the wake of its northern recession, the melting ice left a trough beginning in northeast Tennessee and southwest into the state of Alabama. The 100-mile (160 km) stretch of low land in north Alabama is bound on the north by the southern end of the Cumberland Plateau and on the south by the southern end of the Appalachian Mountains.

Flowing through this trough from northeast Tennessee through north Alabama and west Tennessee into the Ohio River is the Tennessee River.

This river controlled the creation of the vast valley for the purpose of being a drainage basin for the commanding water flow.

Like a dipper, a big bend in the river crosses north Alabama providing a main waterway and rich soil in the valley basin.

Early on, abundant wildlife could be found throughout the area and what better place for the dawn of man.

This Fertile Valley, a wonderful place where natives would thrive long into the future. Studies reveal the existence of man in this area of north Alabama began around 8,000 B.C. The period between 8,000 B.C. – 1,000 B.C. is known as the Archaic Age. The people, named the Paleo Indian, maintained a lifestyle of hunting and gathering natural foods and resources. Settlements were formed along the Tennessee River into the valley and the Warrior Mountains. Around 1,000 B.C. a new tradition began to take shape in the lifestyle of the Archaic Age. The people began to live in more permanent settlements. Their ways of doing things changed.

1,000 B.C. – 1,000 A.D., the Woodland Era is described by the improvement of hunting, gathering and storing of food supplies and the development of towns and formalized leadership structures.

The Tennessee River became a major transportation route and its provision of aquatic plants, mainly freshwater mussels, was an abundant source of food.

The rich soil along the banks of the river and into the valley basin was suitable for farming. Beyond the valley, southward, in the Warrior Mountains, caves and bluffs for shelter could be found.

Therefore it is no surprise that people lived to the west, as the middle course of the Mississippi River began to spread to parts of the southeast.

1,000 A.D. – 1540 A.D., the Mississippian Period became the highest cultural development in North America.

This period of time was marked by the people's involvement in long-distance trade, territoriality and warfare. Highly organized chiefdoms emerged and fortified settlements appeared.

As grand as it was, the Mississippian lifestyle would come to an end. The length of time of habitation in the Tennessee Valley was less than that of the Archaic age or Woodland era.

On June 28, 1540, a white man named Desoto crossed the Tennessee River and entered Alabama. He was the first European to discover the Tennessee River.

Chapter 3

Life in the Valley

The Tennessee Valley climate of sun and rain nurtured the agricultural wealth for the inhabitants.

Indian tribes claiming their territory in the valley considered the land sacred. Like the air we breathe, they believed land could not be bought or sold. Although there was a continuous dispute among the tribes over the Tennessee River waterways and Mussel Shoals, it was not until the arrival of the Europeans in the 1600s that the purchase of land ownership involved the Indian tribes.

Following Desoto's discovery and Indian trails and roads, Europeans found their way to the valley. These people were mostly of Irish descent. As with my family the Irish men married Indian girls and occupied small farms; working their properties with their families.

By the 1900s, there were very few full-blooded Indians living in the valley area. The United States government had forcibly removed most of the Indians to west of the Mississippi River.

Because of the Indian women's inherited survival skills of earlier days and the white man's quest for adventure, the families began to manifest feelings of undiminished identification with the land.

In the late afternoon, Grandpa James, Grandma Lucinda and their children unloaded the wagon and carried their few belongings into the small farmhouse. My great-grandfather John Allen had come to the valley a few years earlier and now found a place for his daughter and her family.

It took only a few minutes for the children to explore the inside of the house, and then they raced to the yard running and playing.

Under warm skies, across a fragrant humid earth, the afternoon shadow covered the narrow porch. Burdened by the displacement of his family, Grandpa James sat on the edge of the porch holding his head in his hands. Sensing the distress of her husband, Grandma Lucinda spoke in a soft but stern voice, "James, this is where we will make our home. We have come to this valley for a reason. Though we are poor in worldly goods, we have been provided a spot on earth where peace, beauty and tranquility abound. A fertile land where crops will grow, our animals will feed and our children will be healthy."

Listening to his wife's words, Grandpa James sensed her spirit of hope. Standing he vowed, "So it is, this valley will be our home. All it will take is hard work and I am used to that. Come Cindy, he called Grandma; let's look for a garden spot."

Life would not be easy, but my ancestors bonded with others in affection for the locale and a sense of "place" on the land of the valley.

Points Of Interest

❖   Warrior Mountains: Name derived from the Muskogee people who lived along the forest streams hundreds of years before white people came to the area. The Creek word "taskagu" or "taska" refer to the English translation of "warrior." The range of mountains: geographic boundary along the Continental Divide. The divide begins by separating the Atlantic's coastal waters from those of the Mississippi drainage in Maine and continues through the upper Tombigbee watershed in the western portion of Alabama and into northern Mississippi. The portion of this chain of mountains that rises from the flat middle plain in the heartland of Lawrence County, Alabama is called the Warrior Mountains.

❖ The Cheatham Trail: An Indian trail: north/south through the Warrior Mountains of northern Alabama. Act of Alabama legislature in 1824 authorized Wyatt Cheatham to build a road along the trail, the route of the present Alabama Highway 33. Also known as the Wilderness Parkway after the Sipsey Wilderness area was established.

❖ The Rose Bush: The rose bush grew by the family garden gate in the 1800s in Jefferson County, Alabama. In 1910, Great, Great, Grandma Martha gave my mother, Rebekah, a cutting from the rose bush and Rebekah planted it by the porch of her home in the forest. It still grows where Rebekah planted it. The story of the rose bush is told in my novel, ***Standing Against the Wind***.

❖ Cherokee Ancestors: In the 1700s treaties were made with the United States government to give up land. In 1830 the Indian Removal Act spelled doom for many Cherokee. My great, great, great, grandma Polly was forced from her homeland in the mountains of the Cumberland Gap and North Carolina. The Treaty of New Echota in 1836 was an attempt to remove all the Cherokee to the west of the Mississippi. Grandma Polly suffered on The Trail of Tears, escaped to live in the Warrior Mountains. My family lived in what is now known as the Bankhead National Forest, North Alabama. They lived there until the early 1900s when the government forced their removal. In 1916, the last of my family left the forest.

❖ The Tennessee Valley: A generally accepted term for North Alabama. It is in reference to the Tennessee River, which flows through the northernmost part of the state of Alabama.

❖ Hernando DeSoto: a Spanish explorer, the first European to move inland to the heart of Indian country.

❖   Date-line Tennessee Valley: Inhabitants

- o   Prehistoric Indians – 8,000 B.C. – 1540 A.D.
- o   Early Historic Indian Tribes and Europeans –
  1540 A. D. – 1800s A.D.
- o   State of Alabama – December 14, 1819

Martha's Parents—Ruben and Velvie Killgore, 1921

Chapter 4

Springtime of 1920

In the spring of 1920 a stranger came to the valley. When the train made its stop in Decatur, Alabama a young man dressed in a suit and tie got off. Standing on the platform, he pulled out his pocket watch, "Excuse me, Sir," he said to a gentleman walking by, "Do you have the correct time? I'm traveling and I'm not sure what time zone I'm in."

With a suspicious look, the man told him the time with a question of his own. "Just passing through, are you?"

"Actually, I'm looking for work. Just came back from the war and I need a job."

After a short conversation, the man, who owned a saw mill, was on his way home with the stranger seated beside him on the wagon seat. He had a job offer and at that time good jobs were hard to find.

This man owned a saw mill but most of the families in the valley were farmers. Their major crop was cotton. The livelihood of most families depended on the success of their cotton crops.

The early settlers of the valley are known for their spirit of willingness to help each other. So it was with the owner of the saw mill, when he asked his newly hired man to go to the neighbor's farm to help work the fields.

A stranger to the valley he was, but not to working the fields. He had been raised on a farm, but often told his family how he hated the farm work. On this day, it was just a paying job and he would think of it as not hard or easy. He just began the plowing. A critical moment in time was about to happen that would determine the path he would follow for the rest of his life.

The early morning April shower had left the red clay soil sticky - and hard for the mule to pull the plow. Grandpa James and his five daughters were doing the best they could in planting the seeds, using a hoe.

Breaking through the clouds a ray of brilliant sunlight blinded the field workers for a few seconds. Wiping the sweat from his brow with his pocket handkerchief, the stranger looked up and out across the plowed field. In the distance he saw a young lady standing between the cotton rows in the red clay. She was wearing a dress that reached her ankles; a bonnet covered her hair.

Uncertain of his footing, each step forward seemed in slow motion. When he got closer, he stopped the mule and looked upon her. Her face opened crimson to the sun. Her lips parted with the freshness of smiles and her eyes sparkled of good humor. Holding her hoe for a brief rest, tilting her bonnet from the rays of the sun, Rebekah's eyes met those of the stranger. Neither of them said a word to each other.

This exchange of glances was noticed by the workers in the field. Immediately the minds of young girls made plans for a fantasy romance. What better way to put their plan into motion than to invite the stranger to the Sunday social at the valley church.

The yard of the Flat Creek Country Church was full of laughter from those enjoying their day of rest; tables of good food and giggling girls.

When he took her hand and said, "My name is Reuben," she now knew his name, but in many ways he would always be a stranger.

They were married December 14, 1920 in the back of the feed store across from the courthouse in Moulton, Alabama. Rebekah, my mother, was eighteen years old. Reuben, my father, said he was twenty five, but later I learned he was thirty-five.

Chapter 5

Great, Great-Grandma Martha

Although my family had settled into their homes in the valley, all ties with the forest had not been severed. Looking forward into the future, Rebekah and Reuben welcomed their first born in the month of October.

Only a few days later, November 12, 1921, the past would over shadow the present. At the age of eighty-two, Great, Great-Grandma Martha died. This Cherokee Indian girl small in stature, black eyes, black hair, never lost her beauty. She followed Great, Great, Great-Grandma Polly in being the matriarch of the family. Maintaining her strength of spirit, she suffered the loss of her first husband in the Civil War, the death of her daughter and the death of her second husband.

Many days would find Martha standing by her husband James grave and daughter, Millie's grave in the family cemetery on Bunyan Hill in the forest. She never saw the resting place of her husband killed during the Civil War.

Horses pulled wagons full of family members up the rocky roads into the forest. So filled with memories, many did not wait till the funeral to shed their tears.

How many days had they worked their fields, tended their gardens, carried for their livestock, cut wood to build their homes and fuel their fires? The children had run their races on the road called Bunyan Hill; the grown-ups sat on their front porches and watched.

In years past, they had been forced to leave this place. Today they returned to bring Great, Great-Grandma Martha to rest beside her loved ones in the Bunyan Hill Cemetery.

Leaving the forest, returning to their home in the valley filled with the spirit of their ancestors, their life on Bunyan Hill Road would never be forgotten. The unspoken words of generations to come, "The forest, will always be our home."

♥♥♥

Reuben's marriage into the family did not change his mind on his discontent for the farm life. He told Rebekah that a man had offered him a job in Indiana. So in 1924 he took his two little boys and wife to live in Indiana.

The story of Reuben's life is told in my book ***Crossing in the Rain.*** The twelve years from 1924-1936 were filled with good times and bad times and the birth of a child every two years increased their family to eight children.

Circumstances of unbelievable situations forced my father to bring my mother and their eight children back to the valley.

It is often said, where do we go when all else fails? We go home. Grandma Lucinda welcomed her daughter with open arms.

Chapter 6

Death of a Brother

Grandpa James never got over his disappointment of having to leave his home in the forest. Some say he lost his mind. Others say he ate some raw sweet potatoes, and then died. It was in September 1927, when the cotton began to bloom in the fields; his work was finished; he was only fifty-four years old.

Grandma Lucinda made the decision not to bury Grandpa in the family cemetery on Bunyan Hill in the forest, but to start a new resting place for her own family. Caddo Church was close to their home in the valley; so it was there that Grandpa James would be the first to be buried in the cemetery beside the small white church.

Rebekah returned from Indiana to attend her father's funeral. In 1931, both Great-Grandma Rhoda and my great-grandpa John Allen passed away. My mother (Rebekah) did not come to the valley for their funerals. It would be five more years before she would come home.

After leaving the forest, Great-Grandpa John Allen prospered in the valley. He was able to leave a sizable inheritance to his children. This enabled Grandma Lucinda to purchase 137 acres of land near Hillsboro, a small town in Lawrence County, near Decatur, Alabama.

Managing her life as best she could after the death of her husband, it was a good choice for her and her children. By now she had five boys living at home. They would be depended on to help Grandma with the corn, sugar cane, and cotton crops. It is amazing how they worked the fields and helped with the vegetable garden and tending to the livestock.

Being only a short distance from the Tennessee River, the land was fertile. A country dirt road ran past the farmhouse to the railroad track and beyond. The daily sound of the train whistle reminded the family of the distant land and a world of which they could only dream.

The arrival of Rebekah, Reuben and their eight children brought excitement and the boys enjoyed the company. Grandma Lucinda was happy to have her oldest daughter back and would see to it that no one went hungry and they had a place to stay. Luckily there was a small house beside the railroad track that was a shack, but Rebekah and her family could stay here until they found something better.

The children were eager to help with the farm chores. Not Reuben, he would seek work in Decatur. Lack of jobs had been my father's reason for leaving this area in 1924, but since then the federal government had organized a corporation called the Tennessee Valley Authority. That, along with the building of the Wilson Dam on the Tennessee River, bolstered the economy in the entire valley area.

Large homes were being built in Decatur, providing my father work as a house painter. Rebekah, as always, helped her mother with the cooking and took care of the young children.

It could have been a joyous time for my family, but tragedy was about to raise its ugly head and life would never be the same for them.

Marion, my oldest brother, Rebekah and Reuben's oldest child, was seriously ill. His suffering began before they moved back to the valley. At one point, he had asked his brothers and sisters and his parents to take a vote to see how many wanted to go home to the valley.

All the votes were "yes." They could not deny their beloved Marion his wish.

May 3, 1937, Marion died. Heartbreak pervaded my grieving family as they stood by his grave in Caddo Cemetery. He was only fifteen years old.

Facts

❖ <u>Cotton Season:</u> During the 1920s, cotton was the major crop of the South. The livelihood of many families depended on the success of their cotton crop. Planting dates in North Alabama – April 20 through May 10. Harvest dates – Mid-September and is completed in mid-December.

❖ <u>Hoes:</u> Early days of growing cotton, the hoe was used. Now the fields are prepared in the spring for planting using a field cultivator or chisel plow and in the fall the fields are tilled with a turning plow.

❖ <u>Pick-sacks:</u> Eight-foot to ten-foot sacks fastened with a strap that goes around the shoulders. Cotton pickers drag these burlap sacks behind them like a giant worm. Now cotton is harvested with a mechanical cotton stripper or a picker machine.

❖ ***Crossing in the Rain***: A book written by the author, Martha Lou Perritti, about Reuben's life (1888-1989)

❖ <u>Rebekah and Reuben meet:</u> page 127 of ***Crossing in the Rain***; page 261 of ***Standing Against the Wind***

❖ <u>Marriage:</u> Rebekah and Reuben, December 14, 1920

❖ <u>Marriage:</u> Great, Great-Grandma Martha and Great, Great-Grandpa William, June 11, 1857

❖ <u>Death:</u> Great, Great-Grandma Martha, November 12, 1921

❖ <u>Death:</u> Great, Great-Grandpa William, Martha's first husband, Confederate soldier, Battle of Mobile Bay, Civil War; died January 7, 1865, buried Magnolia Cemetery, 1202 Virginia Street, Mobile, AL 36604

❖ <u>Death:</u> James, Martha's second husband, died June 21, 1915, buried in Bunyan Hill Cemetery in the forest.

❖ <u>Death:</u> 1927 Grandpa James (1872-1927), Buried Caddo Church Cemetery

❖ <u>Caddo Church Cemetery:</u> In the late 1800s, the settlement called Caddo was established. Located west of Decatur, Alabama; left off Hwy. 24 on Hwy. 327. In the cemetery beside the Caddo Church are the graves of my family members. Grandpa James was the first to be buried here.

❖ <u>Death:</u> 1931, Great-Grandma Rhoda (1865-1931). She was the free-spirited Indian girl born in the forest in 1865. Buried at Maxwell Chapel near Haleyville, Alabama.

❖ <u>Death:</u> 1931, Great-Grandpa John Allen (1858-1931). The son of William, the Confederate soldier who died in the Civil War. Buried at Maxwell Chapel near Haleyville, Alabama.

❖ <u>Maxwell Chapel:</u> Church near Haleyville, Alabama. My great-grandparents died within a few months of each other. Now they rest forever beside each other in this church cemetery.

Historical Facts 1917-1935

❖ 1917 - A. President of United States Woodrow Wilson (1856 – 1924)

❖ The United States enters World War I

❖ 1918 – World War I ends

❖ 1920 – The 19ᵗʰ Amendment gives women the right to vote.

❖ 1921 – President of United States Warren Harding (1865 – 1923), died in office in 1923.

❖ 1923 – President of United States, Calvin Coolidge (1872-1933)

❖ 1929 - A. President of United States, Herbert Hoover (1874-1964)

❖ The stock market crashes, marking the beginning of the Great Depression.

❖ 1933 – President of United States, Franklin D. Roosevelt (1882 - 1945. The only president to serve more than two terms. He was elected to a fourth term, died in office. In 1935, he established a work-relief program, Social Security, and unemployment insurance.

❖ Tennessee Valley Authority: a Federal corporation organized in 1933 to provide cheap electric power, flood control, irrigation, etc. by developing the entire basin of the Tennessee River, esp. by building dams and reservoirs.

❖ Wilson Dam: named after President Woodrow Wilson. Located on the Tennessee River in NW Alabama: 137 feet (48 m) high.

Martha's mother, Velvie McDougle - 1920

Chapter 7

Two Years Later – 1939

Weather-beaten and worn, the old farmhouse stood seemingly abandoned in the middle of a cotton field. Grandma Lucinda opened the front door to welcome her daughter inside.

"The baby is coming," words repeated from daughter to mother and others. Fresh gunnysack sheets were put on the bed; the young boys were hustled out of the room; my mother gripped Grandma Lucinda's hand. "Mama," she said, "this one is not going to be easy." Having given birth to eight babies, Rebekah knew the difference between an easy delivery and a difficult one.

Although Grandma Lucinda had birthed ten children of her own, she was not sure what to do. Things were not going well and she feared for her daughter and the baby.

"Harlace," she called to one of her sons, who was standing in the yard, "You and Harlen hitch the wagon and go get Aunt Josie. Hurry up, tell her the baby is coming."

Early morning frost covered the fields; the muddy dirt road was like glue to the wagon wheels. Aunt Josie lived only one mile away in Fish Pond, but on this day, getting her to the farmhouse, in a hurry, was not going well.

The sixty-year-old midwife prayed out loud when the boys stirred the mules off the road into the open field. Standing like statues, the mules could not pull the wagon any farther.

"Lordy, Lordy," prayed Aunt Josie, "You boys done mired up the wagon." Waving her arms she demanded, "Git me down, that baby is wait'n for Aunt Josie."

The old black woman, with children of her own, walked through the muddy field holding her gingham dress tied up above her knees.

It would have been a comical sight for Harlace and Harlen, except they knew trouble was coming when they had to face Grandma Lucinda.

The field lay bare from the recently harvested crop of cotton as the October season filled the air with the promise of winter.

The fall breeze was warmer than the chill inside the house.

"Mrs. Mac," Aunt Josie called Grandma Lucinda, "Best stoke that fire in the stove. Don't want this baby freezin' to death."

Yes, Aunt Josie was now in charge and everyone was going to be just fine.

The colors of claret and amber trimmed the trees of autumn. Like a shower of scarlet, the leaves fall from their limbs. The whitewashed sky of winter had not arrived; the sun seemed to light the trees like candles.

October 23, 1939; one hundred years had passed since another baby Martha was born. She was my great, great-grandmother. When my mother was asked, what will you name your baby girl?

"I'll name her after her grandmothers, Martha and Lucinda. Her name is Martha Lou."

The reasons I came into this world were not known at birth. I will probably spend my entire life searching for the answer to "why me?"

I learned about my ancestors and can identify with them; I know about the science of DNA; I have studied the solar system and religious beliefs. Nothing explains the wonder of me, what makes me like others, yet all alone with the person of me.

In the arms of my mother, I was protected from the chill in the old farmhouse. There were sounds of laughter from the children coming in and out of the room. With Grandma Lucinda's help, Aunt

Josie prepared to leave. Opening the fold of the blanket for one last baby check, the old black midwife uttered almost to herself, "This child will be fine. She breathes the October air of our valley."

Grandma Lucinda was the first to rock me to sleep, singing the familiar lullaby:

> *"Once upon a time, there were three little birds,*
> *Way up high in the top of a tree*
> *And all day long their funny little song was*
> > *Tweet Tweedle-Dee*
> > *Tweet Tweedle-Dee.*
> *I said to the Mother bird,*
> *What do they eat, that makes them sing so*
> *sweetly to me?*
> *And all she said as she turned her little*
> *head was*
> > *Tweet-Tweedle-Dee*
> > *Tweet-Tweedle-Dee. "*

Home is where my story began with the song of yesterday; the birth of today and the promise of tomorrow. No matter where I go, I will always be From This Fertile Valley.

Chapter 8

Too Young to Remember

My birth certificate filed October 31, 1939, stated: County, Lawrence; town, Hillsboro; state, Alabama; birth date, October 24, 1939, Father and Mother race, white; number children born alive, eight; number born alive but now dead, one; mid-wife, Josie Blalock; Father's age 44; Mother's age 37.

Fifteen years later, in 1954, my father had this certificate amended, changes were made and I don't know the reason why or just what is correct. The one change that was not made and should have been was the age of my father. The secret is revealed in my book, **Crossing in the Rain.**

The facts first written on this certificate didn't matter as the cold winter winds began to blow across the valley. The concerns were to keep wood in the fireplace and the stove in the kitchen; enough food for hungry growing children and quilts to keep them warm as they slept.

Winter days in the Tennessee Valley can be downcast. Grey clouds hovering low over the river basin; rain, sleet and sometimes snow; all preventing the warmth of the sun.

Throughout the country side, coming from their ill-equipped farmhouses, the sounds of children's voices were carried by the wind. No matter the weather, no matter the hardships of the times, it's the children who make the depression fleeting and remind everyone that seasons change and there is always the hope of a brighter tomorrow.

Christmas Day 1939 arrived. Needless to say with eight children, my parents were lucky to have food for a good Christmas dinner, but the one thing that they always had was a Christmas tree. Another delight for the children was under the tree, there were small brown paper sacks; one for each child. The top of the sack was folded down one fold and inside was the same amount for each one; one chocolate drop, one slice of orange candy, one English walnut, one Brazil nut, one apple, one banana, and one orange. If my father could afford it, there would be a jump rope for the girls and a sack of marbles for the boys.

This tradition of the sacks under the tree continued as long as my parents were living. To the children, their sacks were sacred and even though on my first Christmas, I was only an infant, there was a sack with my name on it.

Christmas Day was always a happy time for my family. Yet all the love and laughter on that day in 1939 could not prevent the sorrow that was soon to come.

In February of 1940, Grandma Lucinda went to the town of Moulton, Alabama, to pay her taxes. Ice on the street caused her to slip, fall, and break her hip. She was treated by a doctor in Moulton, and then sent home. Lying in her bed for months, she lost her will to live and refused to eat.

In the afternoon, on June 23, 1940, the family gathered round the farmhouse. Farmers hoeing the cotton fields quit and came to the yard.

Born in the forest of the Warrior Mountains, daughter of a Cherokee mother; Lucinda had endured the struggles of living through the removal of her family to the valley. On this day of her death, the people of the Tennessee Valley would mourn and her ten children grieved.

My sister held me in her arms as Grandma lay dying on the bed. All my life I would be reminded of Grandma's last words, "Take care of my little Martha Lou." I was too young to remember.

Chapter 9

Move to Jacksonville – Back to Valley

Thirteen years had passed since Grandpa James died and left Grandma Lucinda with five young boys still living at home with her. Their five daughters were married with homes of their own.

Fortified with the knowledge from her ancestors, maintaining her strength of endurance and graced with the presence of her faith; Grandma Lucinda raised her boys; some say with a stern fist. But, without her guidance, the boys soon lost control of the farm. The day they buried Grandma Lucinda, next to her husband in the Caddo Church Cemetery, was the beginning of the end of their life in the valley.

The relationship between my father and the boys was strained. Therefore, when a man from my father's past offered him a job in Jacksonville, Florida, he jumped at the chance to move out of the valley.

I am told that life was good for my family in Jacksonville. We lived on a small farm. My mother had a large vegetable garden and there were several different farm animals.

Seems as though my favorite pasttime was chasing the chickens around the yard and playing with their watering jars. One day, Father caught me at my game and was going to spank me, but one of my sisters picked me up and begged him not to. Father didn't spank me on that day and I don't remember him ever hitting me.

I don't recall the chicken incident, but it has since been brought to my attention from several siblings that because Daddy never hit me I was a spoiled person. I say the jury is still out on that one!

In Jacksonville, there was another sack added under the Christmas tree. Mother had her tenth and last child when she was forty years old. The remaining years of her life would be spent in total dedication to her children.

Realizing her brothers were struggling to hold onto the family farm in the valley, it came as no surprise when one of them pleaded with her to come back to the farmhouse and take over. It was a tough decision for my parents to make, but the dark days of war now shrouded over the country and sacrifices had to be made. All of Mother's brothers enlisted in the armed services.

The train that carried my family to Jacksonville now brought them back to the valley. How could it be that this valley was so peaceful when the ugly head of evil had created a world of war?

The year I was born, 1939, a man named Adolf Hitler of Germany began his march through Europe. Britain and France declared war on Germany but at this point the United States considered it a foreign war and would wait and see. When the bombs fell on Pearl Harbor from an attack by Japan, our wait for war was over. It had come to our door.

My Uncle Obie picked us up at the train station. Cousin James drove a second wagon and most of the eight children rode in his wagon. This was the first time I remember seeing horses pull a wagon and I felt sorry for them having to work so hard pulling the wagon from Trinity to the top of Caddo Mountain. From there the journey was slow, as the country dirt road meandered down the hillside.

Returning to the valley; smell the honeysuckle vine and stop for a drink from the sweet spring water that runs from the forest. Listen for the call of the whippoorwill from the trees and the clatter of the crickets from the thickets alongside the road. Take heed to the wind for the sound of the train. Cross the track cautiously and revel in the sight of the bounty of wild flowers along the way. Notice the trees on the right side of the road, a field of white cotton on the other. Turn onto the short path that leads to the clean swept yard of a weather-beaten farmhouse with clapboard siding and a rusty tin roof. "Grandma's

Place," where I was born.

At age four, I did not realize the desolate situation my family was facing. My father had no intention of staying on the farm. He left us and went to live in Birmingham where he worked as a painter. Gone for months at a time, he provided no support to my mother. These were turbulent years for my mother.

Unyielding to the fact that her family was considered to be poor, my mother drew from the strength of her ancestors the courage to go forward. She taught her children the value of hard work and maintaining our faith in God.

My memory of these years on the farm comes in bits and pieces. My favorite place to play was in the northeast corner of my mother's vegetable garden, next to the wood pile. When I asked Mother about the bright green plants that grew there, she seemed angry when she answered, "I don't know why these things keep growing there. They are herbs your grandmother used for healing, but they sure didn't save her life."

Mother never talked to me about Grandma Lucinda. In fact, she never joined in the family story telling. On Sunday afternoons different members of the family: aunts, uncles, cousins, would gather round the porch and tell stories. One of my cousins played a guitar and everyone would join in on the singing.

Hot, summer days were good for laying a quilt out under the enormous tree that shaded the front yard. Those were the days I first used my imagination. Lying on that quilt, looking up at the clouds, watching them form different shapes; this was during the day, then at night Mother would let me stay up until the stars came out and I could be mesmerized by the dark sky and bright shining stars.

Fighting and arguing among my siblings always calmed down when Father showed up. Mother's presence was always loving and understanding and everyone took good care of me.

Usually when I asked one of my sisters to take me to visit Aunt Rhoda, they would check with Mother and we would be on our way. It is no wonder that my aunt Rhoda was my favorite person in the whole world. She treated me special; making popcorn and rolling it in molasses to form popcorn balls; showing me the pretty cloth for making dresses she had put away in her trunk under her bed; and when I was allowed to stay overnight, Aunt Rhoda tucked me into bed under pretty, warm quilts.

The story is told, but only one part of it remains clear in my mind: On a warm day in late spring, I was outside playing in the yard. I was barefoot and had on a cotton dress that Mother made. After several attempts to get one of my sisters to go with me to Aunt Rhoda's place, I decided to go by myself.

It was about a mile down the dirt road, across the railroad track from "Grandma's Place" to Aunt Rhoda's place. Mother lived in fear of one of her children getting hit by the train, because it was only a country road crossing with no signal to warn of an oncoming train. Most of the time, train conductors would sound the whistle before they got to the crossing. Mother knew the times for the train by heart.

Of course, none of this was considered in my child's mind as I left the yard, went down the path to the dirt road and walked toward the railroad track. Unaware of any dangers ahead, I skipped along playfully, stopping to pick up small sticks, rocks or objects of interest. This is the part that I clearly remember. Looking across the narrow ditch of the road, I saw a patch of wildflowers. They were mixed with the bright and dark shades of springtime green, with colors of orange, yellow, red, blue and white scattered about like pepper. Just as I was about to step into the flowers, my eyes caught the folds of a skirt brushing the blooms. I raised my eyes to see the most beautiful lady standing there in the middle of the wildflower patch.

Her long dress was sheer organdy, pale blue like the sky and frail to see. She wore a wide brim hat with a band of ribbon streamers that tossed in the breeze. Resting on her arm was a basket laden with gathered flowers.

-The years have not diminished the sound of her voice-

"Come little girl, will you help me pick the flowers?" She sat her basket down so I could reach it.

I was not afraid of her and although I was usually shy with strangers, I began to ask her questions. "Are you lonely out here all by yourself? Are these your flowers? Do you live here? Who are you picking the flowers for?"

With a smile, she spoke softly, "No, I'm not lonely. I've been waiting for you and I picked this clover to make a necklace for you to wear."

I picked the clover from her basket and the beautiful lady gracefully tied the stems. She hung the finished strand around my neck, saying, "You are a beautiful little girl."

I asked her, "Am I as pretty as you?"

Looking into my eyes, stroking my hair, her words were, "Someday you will be me. Now you must go to Aunt Rhoda's, she's looking for you."

I crossed the ditch and when I looked back I saw only the field of wildflowers. I don't remember the train going by.

Mother was taking clothes off the clothesline when she heard the whistle of the 2:00 p.m. train. When she noticed I was not in the yard, she called out to some of the other children, "Where is Martha Lou?"

I was missing and when the girls told Mother I had asked them to take me to visit Aunt Rhoda, she was afraid that her worst nightmare had come true. She and the children ran toward the railroad track.

Crossing the track, they saw no signs to worry, but when they arrived at Aunt Rhoda's to see me standing behind her, most of them were furious with me.

Mother didn't have much to say, just told me not to ever run away like that again. "You must never leave the yard alone," she said.

I told her I was not alone, that I was with a beautiful lady and we picked flowers. I don't believe anyone ever believed that I saw or was with this mysterious lady, but no one could explain the clover necklace I was wearing around my neck.

If the beautiful lady was just a childhood fantasy, why have I seen her two other times during my life?

Facts

❖ Birth Certificate: October 23, 1939, Lawrence County, Alabama; town, Hillsboro, "Grandma's Place," located closer to a community called Fish Pond than Hillsboro.

❖ Lawrence County is a northern Alabama county created on February 4, 1818 and named in honor of the famous naval hero, Captain James Lawrence. Locals tend to refer to the area as the "Tennessee Valley" in reference to the Tennessee River, which flows north of the county.

❖ Hillsboro and Fish Pond remain small communities while the city of Decatur is considered the quasi-anchor city for the area.

❖ Fish Pond – a place dear to my heart as I remember all the stories told: legend is the pond is bottomless, a body of water where you can catch four and five pound catfish and the best swimming hole in the valley. The rural community that surrounds the pond, some say "just a wide spot in the road," today has a few homes and businesses and two churches. Mr. Cantrell's grocery store is where I found my first penny!

❖ Decatur, Alabama is nicknamed "The Heart of the Valley" because of its location near the exact center of the length of the Tennessee River. Vital to the economic landscape of North Alabama, most of the north/south shipping traffic is funneled through the town utilizing three river crossings that are main routes for rail and road traffic between Birmingham and Nashville, Tennessee.

❖ Grandma's House - The flat fertile land of the valley surrounded this small, wood framed, tin roofed, farmhouse. Two steps up to the front porch that reached across the front of the house. The front door opened into a large room, fireplace on right side; two beds to the left. Between the two beds a door into a side room where the older girls slept. At the back of the large front room a doorway into the kitchen. Directly in front of the doorway a wood burning kitchen stove; to the left a long table with benches. There were two small windows on each end of the kitchen. The back door by the kitchen table opened out onto a small stoop.

❖ Beside the peach tree in the back yard, stood a tin-roofed smokehouse. The smokehouse was used for storing meat and different vegetables during the winter months. The children would slice the peaches and put them on the tin roof of the smokehouse for them to dry. From these dried peaches, Mother made fried peach pies.

❖ About 500 feet from the back of the house a pond is surrounded by a thicket of trees and underbrush where blueberries grow.

Near the pond stands a huge tree its branches stretching almost as wide as the pond.

❖ A place where family memories are made and fade away as the wind blows the blooms from the cottonwood tree in the front yard. The blooms that look like cotton end with the season and the final season came for the cottonwood tree, the smokehouse and the farmhouse. Only the pond and large tree remained after Grandma's Place disappeared from the landscape of the valley.

❖ Grandma Lucinda – Born 1883 in the forest of the Warrior Mountains, Died 1940 in the Tennessee Valley. The story of her fifty seven years of life is told in the author's book **Standing Against the Wind**.

❖ Gunny sack – A sack made of coarse, heavy fabric of jute or hemp. Often used for animal food, seeds and other dry goods. Grandma Lucinda pulled the thread used to sew the sack together. Each sack became about one yard of material. The gunny sack material was placed in a wash pot of boiling water. Usually the lettering on the sack would not come out. Grandma made shirts, underwear and sheets using the gunny sack material. It was these gunny sack sheets that were on the bed where my mother gave birth to me.

❖ Storytelling – Oral literature encompassed the whole identity of the people, their philosophy, their history- not just for entertainment; it was the whole basis of community.

❖ Christmas sacks – small paper sacks filled with candy, especially a chocolate drop, and fruit. The amount and what the candy and fruit was depended on what my parents could afford at the time. One sack for each child; placed underneath the Christmas tree by "Santa Claus." This tradition continued as long as my parents lived.

- ❖ **World War II** – After Germany invaded Poland, Britain and France declared war on Germany in September 1939. The war became world wide when Japan and Italy join Germany to form the Axis Powers. The Japanese attacked Pearl Harbor, Hawaii on December 7, 1941 causing the United States to declare war on Japan. The Axis then declared war on the United States.
  - The Soviet Union joined the United States and other Allied nations. On June 6, 1944 – D- Day- Allied forces crossed the English Channel and landed in western France. During this time, the Soviet troops were advancing on Germany from the East. The U.S. forces had defeated the Axis troops in North Africa and had invaded Italy. These actions combined forced Germany to surrender on May 7, 1945.
  - The U.S. battled Japan on the islands of the Pacific Ocean. Atom bombs dropped on Hiroshima and Nagasaki forced Japan to surrender on August 14, 1945.
  - The war began in 1939 and ended in 1945. Bombs on Pearl Harbor started it for the U.S. A bigger bomb dropped by the U.S. ended it.
- ❖ Franklin Delano Roosevelt – President of the United States 1933-1945. During his first term in office, he guided the United States out of the deep Depression. The U.S. was at war during his second term. He was elected to a third term in 1944 but died before the war ended in 1945.

❖   *"Tweet – Tweedle – Dee"* – A lullaby, a mother's song, remembered
    from one generation to the next. My sister Inez gave me the
    words:

> *"Once upon a time, there were*
> *three little birds.*
> *Way up high in the top of a*
> *tree.*
> *And all the day long their funny*
> *Little song was Tweet-Tweedle-Dee*
> *Tweet-Tweedle-Dee*
> *I said to the Mother bird,*
> *What do they eat, that makes them*
> *sing so sweetly to me?*
> *And all she said as she turned her*
> *little head was*
> *Tweet-Tweedle-Dee*
> *Tweet-Tweedle-Dee."*

❖   <u>The beautiful lady by the railroad tracks</u> – There was never any
    proof that this lady existed. Yet I have seen this lady three times
    during my lifetime!

Chapter 10

Good-Bye to Grandma's Place

"In the pines, in the pines, where the sun never shines, and you shiver when the cold wind blows"

Country Song

In the shade of the trees that surrounded the pond; had been my mother's place of refuge. There is where she could be alone; pray aloud in her thanksgiving for God's blessings; seeking His guidance in decisions to be made.

Only in this place she felt so close to nature and to her ancestors. Mother shivered from the chill as the wind blew through the trees; she left her burdens by the pond; returning to care for her children.

She walked out of the woods into the sunlight with the promise from my father to provide a better life for her and their children.

Father bought a house in Pinson, Alabama, a suburb of Birmingham. Mother sold Grandma's Place.

At this time, I was about five years old, the same age as my great, great, great Cherokee grandmother when she left her birthplace in the Cumberland Gap.

Because my great, great, great-grandmother was Cherokee Indian, she was forced to move with her tribe. The United States government broke treaties and continued to push the Native American south from the Cumberland Gap into the foothills of the Smoky Mountains of North Carolina.

Still not satisfied, in 1838, the United States government declared that all Native Americans east of the Mississippi River would relocate in the state of Oklahoma. By this time, Grandmother Polly was married to a Scotch-Irish man and had two boys.

They were living a peaceful life in Gwinnett County, Georgia. Grandmother Polly tended her garden while the boys played nearby. Grandfather was away on a trip to Atlanta. Union soldiers raided their home, forcing Grandmother and the two young boys to join other Cherokee Indians on what is now know as "The Trail of Tears."

Held in a stockade in Fort Payne, Alabama, Grandmother and the boys survived until Grandfather rescued them and they fled into the Warrior Mountains of North Alabama.

One of these small boys, William, became my great, great-grandfather. He married a Cherokee girl, Martha, and their son, John Allen, was my great-grandfather. John Allen also married a Cherokee girl, Rhoda.

Lands of the Warrior Mountains were the home of my family for seventy-eight years. My grandmother Lucinda was born there, my mother was born there.

The authorities of the United States government were not finished with this family. In the early 1900s, the government began to force them to move out of the Warrior Mountains to make way for a national forest.

Moving down out of the forest, my ancestors settled in the farmland of what is known as "The Tennessee Valley."

A story is told about an Indian shaman named Three Feathers, who began to live with my family during "The Trail of Tears" until he went to be with my great, great-grandfather William fighting in the Civil War.

Grandfather William was a Confederate soldier and died in the battle of Mobile Bay. It is believed that the body of Three Feathers died on that day in 1864, but the Spirit of Three Feathers lives on in the forest of the Warrior Mountains.

This story is real to me, because I know the spirits of my ancestors shroud the country side of the Tennessee Valley.

My father found his way to this place; married my mother and I was born. The wonder of Grandma's Place will always be a part of me and the ties will always bind me to this fertile valley.

Leaving Grandma's place, I began my life's journey.

Martha Lou, 1946 - Pinson, Alabama

Chapter 11

Pinson

I remember our house in Pinson being comfortable and, as promised, my father put me up a swing under a large tree in the front yard.

It was in this swing I could escape from my siblings and dream of my life to be.

Father worked as a painter in Birmingham and didn't always come home at night. When he was home, I was fascinated by the pocket watch he wore. The chain hooked to his belt; the watch sliding into a little pocket of his pants. Sometimes Father would hold the watch to my ear and let me hear it tick.

"With each tick, that means time is passing," Father said. "You can't get back the tick that just passed and you can't change the tick forward. Time is all measured by this tick."

Throughout my life, this time with my father was very meaningful to me. Before he passed away at age 101, he gave me his pocket watch. Now my son has it. This same watch still ticks!

Memories of Pinson: Mother washing clothes in a spring that ran along the bottom of a small hill behind our house; Mother hanging the clothes on the bushes for them to dry; seeing a tornado as it churned its way toward our house while we crouched in a storm cellar; coming out of the storm cellar to see the roof of our house completely gone and wind and rain had destroyed most of our belongings. Vivid memories include:

--Starting to school in the first grade, I learned all the letters of the alphabet and how to write. I loved writing even then.

--My sister using chalk to mark on the back door steps. Depicting the keys of a piano; trying to practice her piano lessons. My parents were too poor to buy a piano. The piano lessons were free in the school.

--Walking home from the school bus. Sometimes on the dirt road; other times through the forest of trees. One day I chose the tree route during a terrible rain storm, poor choice!

--Gathering up books from around the house; stacking them and pretending I could read all of them. To my amazement I discovered that people wrote these books. How could a person write all these words? How could that be? When I grow up, will I be able to write a whole book?

The first five of my schooling years were turbulent times for my family. I did not understand anything that was going on with my parents. I just remember going to school wherever we were living.

First in Pinson; then in Trinity, Alabama, where we lived with a sister and her husband; then in Hartselle, Alabama, where we lived in a southern mansion, then moved to a country shack.

From the time we left Grandma's place in 1945 until we moved into the country shack near Hartselle, several of my siblings married, went into the military or just left home to live elsewhere.

By 1950, there were only three children left living with my mother and our lives were about to change forever.

"The day dreams I had while I was swinging in the swings Father made for me when I was five, six, seven, eight years old; I have made most of those dreams come true!"

PART
II

Martha Lou – 1958
High School, Orlando, Florida

Chapter 12

Orlando, Florida - 1950

I don't want to sound disrespectful of my birthplace, the Tennessee Valley of North Alabama, but because of my father's vision of a better life for me, he relocated our family to Orlando, Florida.

Leaving the country shack; boarding a Greyhound bus with my few belongings in a cardboard box stored in the baggage holder underneath the bus; it was like running away from a sad dream. Arriving at my final destination, the doors to the bus opened and I stepped out into a new world, Orlando, the City Beautiful, Florida, the Sunshine State.

The year was 1950 and even then it felt like Disney World to me. Many times during my father's life I thanked him for bringing me to Orlando. The entire livelihood of my family improved.

Our neighborhood was middle class; West Central Grammar School was in walking distance and provided me with many childhood opportunities. Such as: belonging to the Girl Scouts, singing in the school choir, becoming a spelling bee champion and an abundance of new friendships.

For many years I kept the white dress that I wore to my grammar school graduation. This was the first graduation of one of his children that my father attended. There would be many more for me and he attended them all.

Memorial Junior High School was located by Lake Eola, a landmark in the middle of Orlando. My thoughts swell with joy, pride, and gratefulness as I remember the three years in attendance there; getting three awards for not missing a single day of school for three years.

Drama class, starring in plays on stage; speech class, learning how to debate and give lectures; marching with the school band, proudly wearing my soldierette suit; first year of a foreign language, Spanish; enjoying all my friendships, parties, football games, sodas at the corner drugstore (it was the '50s); having lots of boyfriends, going "steady" with a few; that was junior high.

Middle of the 1950s, Father moved us into a house on Amelia Street – downtown Orlando. By now there were only two children left living with Father and Mother. I had my own bedroom!

At the time I didn't realize it and just now, in my later years, have I come to realize that these years living on Amelia Street molded me into the adult person I became. Many hours I spent with my father, listening to his advice, encouragement and many stories.

"You are very smart," he told me, "different from the others. Get all the education you can. No one can ever take what you learn away from you."

Father was home every night, helping me with my homework, allowing me to enjoy my social life. My siblings have said my daddy spoiled me. He let me have friends, date boys, go to parties, etc. I guess they have a problem with my relationship with Father. I was with him the day he died at age 101 and I don't regret one day of listening to what he had to say.

Throughout my teenage years, my mother remained occupied with helping all her children. I understand their need of her and now remember my special times with her; going to church on Sunday morning and when I came home from school in the afternoon opening the door and calling out, "Mom." She always answered.

Sister Inez hosted a celebration of my sixteenth birthday. Photos are proof of the joyous occasion I shared with my many friends and the loving kindness of my sister.

1955 – 1958 I call my wonder years. I wondered if I was smart enough, pretty, talented, what my boyfriends were thinking, did I fit in with this group or that group, and constantly I wondered what I should wear. All these wonders seemed to take care of themselves as I consistently made the honor roll with my grades; became a member of the speaking debate team; acted in drama plays with the theater group; broadcast our school news on the local radio station; had many boyfriends (which I took to mean I was pretty enough) and I hung out with each of the different groups: popular, unnoticed, and nerds.

My graduating class of 1958 of Edgewater High School produced some of the greatest citizens of the United States. Their talents have been spread all over the country and beyond; doctors, lawyers, judges, politicians, teachers, scientists, and I add myself to the mix as an author.

A friend of mine attributed these many successes to the teachers we had at Edgewater. I add to this extra ordinary education the facts of the times:

Places, Events Of My Life – 1950's
Orlando, Florida

❖ Motto: "Built for Families, Made for Memories" is the best description I can provide for the lifestyle impact this city had on my family. Arriving on the scene in 1950, I found Orlando not to be as my father had described it as "Just a wide place in the road" when he was there in 1918. On the contrary, Orlando was now truly "The City Beautiful."

❖ The countryside slopes were covered with bright-green trees bearing golden colored oranges. Small blue-water lakes dotted the landscape every few miles. The streets were clean of any debris and the delightful warmth of the sun made my body feel good.

❖ Located in the central region of the state of Florida, Orlando's history begins with the Spaniard Ponce de Leon; seeking a mythical "Fountain of Youth" discovered and named Florida. Thus in 1513 Spain claimed its ownership but was often disputed by the English. In the year 1819 Spain sold Florida to the United States.

❖ The 19th century was marked by wars with the Seminole Indians. 1842 brought the end of the conflict in Central Florida. The Seminoles were pushed south and war continued until 1858. The Seminoles never surrendered.

❖ After 1842, settlers followed soldiers into Central Florida and a settlement grew around an old army base. Some say the name Orlando came from a soldier named Orlando Reeves. He died in the area during the war against the Seminole Indians.

❖ Others say Orlando Reeves operated a sugar mill and plantation and pioneer settlers simply found his name carved into a tree and assumed it was a marker for his grave site. People referred to the area as "Orlando's grave" and later just "Orlando." Either way, the name remained until today.

❖ Until 1880 Central Florida was mainly cattle raising country. Then the railroad came to Orlando and the citrus industry rapidly expanded because the railway provided access to northern markets.

❖ By the end of World War I, 1918, this inland city had become a popular resort area. A housing boom was experienced in the 1920s but came to a halt during the depression years of the 1930s.

❖ World War II, 1939-1945, a number of Army personnel were stationed at the two military bases: Orlando Army Air Base and Pinecastle Army Air Field.

❖ Ironically, servicemen staying in the area with their families first brought progressive settlement to Orlando and once again after

World War II soldiers provided population growth with a renewed economy.

❖ Even so by the year 1950, Orlando had not yet experienced the burgeoning commercial and population it was destined to have in the future.

❖ Harry S. Truman (1884-1972) The 33rd president of the United States; serving from 1945-1953. He authorized dropping the new atomic bomb on Japan, an action that quickly ended World War II.

❖ In 1950, he sent U.S. troops to stop the invasion of South Korea by communist North Korea. He strongly supported halting Soviet expansion and policies were put into place that began a long struggle between the United States and the Soviet Union, called the Cold War.

❖ Dwight D. Eisenhower (1890-1969): President of the United States 1953-1961. A military leader during World War II, he worked hard to achieve peace. In 1953, he negotiated an end to the Korean conflict. Although 2008, 55 years later, U.S. troops still remain in South Korea.

❖ Firmly against communism, he broke off diplomatic relations with Cuba, which had become communist under the dictator Fidel Castro.

❖ President Eisenhower remained enormously popular both before and after his election because of his bravery, integrity, warmth, and sincerity.

❖ Atomic Bomb: The first nuclear bomb developed by the United States government's top secret Manhattan Project. Its power resulted from the immense quantity of energy suddenly released, when a very rapid chain reaction of nuclear fission is set off.

❖ First used in warfare August 6, 1945, by the United States against the Japanese to end the war.

❖ <u>Television</u>: Just as the invention of the atomic bomb changed our lives forever, so did the invention of television. Vladimir Zworykin is credited with demonstrating the first workable television system in 1929.

❖ By the 1950s, television in people's homes had taken center stage. From 1945 to 1960, the number of television sets in the United States rose from 10,000 to 60 million.

❖ In the year 2008, 98 percent of all households in the United States had at least one television set. This is the most popular form of communication and entertainment in the United States.

❖ Viewing of the news, commercials, presidential debates, movies, concerts and more, all impact our society's culture. In the 1950s, my father's favorite shows were "Gunsmoke" and "The Ed Sullivan Show."

❖ I remember watching "The Ed Sullivan Show" with Father when Elvis Presley made his first appearance. I was a teenager who was mesmerized. Father's only comment, "The boy can sing!" For young and old, television changed our lives.

❖ **1954-Attack on Polio**- Tens of thousands came down with the polio disease. Many died, others were left paralyzed.

❖ In 1954, researcher Jonas Salk put a new vaccine to the test with tremendous results. By 1961, when an oral vaccine was introduced, the dreaded polio was almost gone.

❖ <u>**Mother's Faith**</u>: Mother was a member of a Baptist church and we attended church most every Sunday. One of the most memorable moments of my life is when the pastor of our church baptized me.

❖ Mother and others stood on the shores of Lake Lorna Doone as the pastor led me into the water. I remember looking up toward the sky and in the clouds I saw "her," the beautiful lady with the pale blue dress; almost transparent. The snow-white clouds folded over her as I was lowered into the water. Only a few minutes passed until I was back on shore with Mother wrapping me in a warm towel. I don't remember a thing the pastor said. From then on I was considered a member of the Baptist faith.

❖ <u>Father's Secret</u>: Without my knowledge, at the time, in 1954, Father had my birth certificate amended. What was that all about? Read my book "***Crossing in the Rain,***" the secret life of my father.

Martha Lou & her mother Velvie Killgore, 1960 – Orlando, Florida

Chapter 13

What Comes

Next

"Lonely" is the word for me after my high school graduation. My best friends all went away to college. College was not something my father could afford. Luckily he did know a rich man, Mr. King, who was willing to loan me the six hundred dollar tuition needed to attend Jones Business College located in downtown Orlando.

Standing in the doorway of my bedroom, Father asked if he could come in. It was the only time I remember him ever being in my bedroom. I was about to experience what I call "the grown-up talk."

"Martha," he said, "If you will go to this business college, don't try to work and go to school at the same time. This room is yours for as long as you live at home. I will give you spending money as long as you are in school. Then, when you start working, you can give your mother money if you want to. I am proud of you for having graduated from high school and always making good grades and for being a child your mother and I could always trust."

"Thank you, Dad," was all I could say before he left my room. I lifted the lid to the beautiful cedar chest that Father had given me for my graduation gift. They call it a "Hope Chest." I call it my "Dream Chest," either one, from that day forward I filled it with hopes and dreams.

Loneliness disappeared as I set sail on a course for my future, college, a job and whatever would come next!

Father witnessed my graduation from Jones Business College on a Friday night in 1960 and I started my first job on Monday morning.

Turner-Haack Restaurant Equipment Company; position, bookkeeper; five days a week from 8:00 a.m. til 5:00 p.m.; forty-five dollars a week; the description of a time that summed-up my life to that point and opened the door to my future.

Beginning with the job interview; Mr. Haack, the owner of the company, was a little scary and I was very nervous, but soon he became my mentor and it didn't hurt that his son was a handsome boy I knew from high school.

During these years at Turner-Haack, I bought my first car; voted for the president of the United States for my first time to vote; watched the television set then ran outside to see the space capsule carrying Alan B. Shepard, Jr., the first American in space (from their launching on the east coast of Florida the space craft can be seen in the sky over Orlando).

Martha Lou and her first car

My life was filled with all these events, but like every young lady, I spent most of my time dreaming and searching for my "Prince Charming."

Jones Business College Graduation – Orlando, Florida 1960

After I graduated from high school, Father agreed to my dating boys that were stationed at the military bases near Orlando. All my boyfriends from high school I had known most of my life; these boys in the military came from all over the United States. Their lives were so interesting and I enjoyed the dances held at the military bases and activities at the USO club in Orlando.

The only negative aspect was the friendships lasted for only a short time due to the transfers.

Memories of these times: working, driving around town in my new car when gasoline was twenty two cents a gallon, dating military men, many wonderful memories and it is great when your memory doesn't fail you. It can be nerve-racking, disappointing and even embarrassing when you try to remember a particular time or in my case "date." I mean "date" as in the day of the year.

Now, the "date" as in girl meets boy, I remember vividly.

Chapter 14
Martha Lou Meets Frank

I have no recollection as to the date, month, day of the week; just that it was early in the evening, the first time I saw Frank. "A blind date," it is called when a friend says please go out with this person because he has a car and it is the only way I can have a date with his friend.

By agreeing to this proposition, I met the person with whom I was to spend the next forty-six years of my life. Although, of course, it took Frank and me three years after this first meeting to figure out we were no longer going to be alone on life's road we were traveling. Wherever the destination, we would be together.

March 17, 1962 – I became a military wife.

My marriage came with a warning. Father Antos, the navy military chaplain of the United States Naval Air Station, Sanford, Florida, lectured me for one hour a day, for five days. I figured the timing was designed to let the topic discussed soak in before the next session and to give me a chance with excuse to run!

At first I was reluctant to sit and listen to Father Antos, but when Frank proposed marriage to me, he said I must understand that in our marriage the duties of the Navy man will come first, before his duties as my husband.

I needed to understand his reasoning behind this statement and Father Antos was there to tell me all I needed to know:

Frank Victor Perritti leaving for the Mediterranean Sea
August 4, 1960

Mr. & Mrs. Frank Victor Perritti, Jr.
Wedding Day – 1962

Frank's job is dangerous. Sometimes you won't hear from him for long periods of time Neither he nor you will have control over where you live.

At all times you must be prepared to pack and unpack quickly. You may be moving by yourself because Frank can be out to sea for months at a time.

Handling "at home" crises will be your responsibility. From fixing toilets, changing oil in the car, fertilizing the lawn, even dealing with natural disasters such as hurricanes; you are on your own.

It will do you no good to get upset to see other husbands coming home from work everyday.

You can't count on Frank being with you on holidays, even Christmas, birthdays and anniversaries.

Don't count on him being there when you have the babies.

There will be many times when the feeling of being alone will overwhelm you.

"Martha Lou," Father Antos called me, "If you can handle all these things with grace and dignity, you will be a good military wife. If you can handle all these things while hiding the tears, you will be a needed example for others."

I didn't count these facts because there were so many more to be added later.

My last session with Father Antos, he said to me, "Do you still want to marry Frank?"

My reply, "Yes, I do. I love him."

"Okay," he said, "After this marriage ceremony, don't come back to me crying that you can't take it. Don't ruin this young man's career."

I am pleased to say after forty-six years of "this marriage," I have never cried to anyone about my husband's career. After all, I was warned!

Chapter 15

One Step Behind

Life has a way of bringing two people together, vowing to love, honor and protect, as long as they live. Standing in front of family members and friends before the altar of the military chapel, Sanford Naval Air Station; Father Antos pronounced Frank and me man and wife.

I turned to walk down the aisle, the same aisle I had walked down only minutes before. I had slowly walked the aisle alone; this time was different. Frank and I held hands as we rushed toward the door.

Together we stepped out of the doorway into what seemed like a whole new world. I was now on my husband's career path. My destiny to be a military wife had begun. My commitment was to follow that path, one step behind.

I realized there would be sacrifices on my part, just as Frank had pledged when he joined the Navy. I too would serve our country to protect our freedom.

Married only a couple of weeks; Frank left to be gone four months on an aircraft carrier. We had rented a small house in Orlando and I continued my job at Turner-Haack Company.

I did have worrisome concerns about Frank's safety as I was aware that he handled weapons aboard the ship.

The concerns became terrifying moments when after he returned from four months at sea, the knock at the door was notifying Frank to return to base immediately. We were going to war!

President John F. Kennedy ordered a naval blockade of Cuba because the Soviet Union had built missile launch sites in Cuba. Living

Richard, Martha Lou & Frank Perritti, Jr.

in Florida, so close to Cuba, we knew if a nuclear missile was launched from Cuba it would destroy us and many other cities in the United States.

Frank was aboard the aircraft carrier USS Independence as they held the "at ready." President Kennedy demanded the Soviet Union to remove the missiles. Nikita Khrushchev, premier of the Soviet Union, refused.

Six days passed, as the whole world braced itself for a nuclear war. On October 28, 1962, Khrushchev began to pull the missiles out of Cuba and destroy the launch sites. The United States agreed not to invade Cuba.

The Cuban Crisis was over, Frank could come home, that is for this time. Married to a military man for less than a year, I recognized this must be an ongoing commitment. Feeling alone, lonely and afraid, at first; I soon realized that I had joined the ranks of military wives who are some of the strongest women in the world.

Military wives before me had survived these challenges. They held their families together, were always there, they loved their husbands and I loved this person I call Frank.

Shortly after the Cuban Missile Crisis, Frank received orders that he would be stationed at the Sanford Naval Air Station, Sanford, Florida for shore duty. We were excited. This meant we could buy a house, start our family. Frank would be home for awhile.

We settled into what seemed to be a "normal" life. After moving into our home in Altamonte Springs, Florida, I began working as a bookkeeper for the Suburban Propane Gas Company.

"Are you pregnant?" asked the president of the company.

"Do you plan to become pregnant anytime soon? I don't want to hire you, then have you quit in a couple of months because you are having a baby."

(Those were the days if you had a baby you didn't work away from the house.)

"No, sir." I was adamant to both questions.

Sitting at my desk wearing what was a fashionable sack dress with large buttons all down the side, I turned in my chair to reach my cup of morning coffee.

"Ping, ping, ping," the large brown button skipped across the office floor, followed with giggles from my co-workers.

Looking down at my expanding waistline, I was not surprised when the boss called out, "Martha, in my office please."

Needless to say my career with the gas company was short lived. Our baby was coming!

Chapter 16

Birth and Death

Because we lived close to my family in Orlando, we did most of our socializing with family members. I had very little contact with other military wives.

Hovering over me like a mother hen, my sister Mildred was the most supportive. She had six children of her own, so I figured advice from her came from experience.

Dr. Smith assured me that I was healthy, the baby was healthy and he told Frank to stop worrying. Forty-five years later the baby and I remain healthy; Frank still worries!

One event he didn't seem too concerned about is that he would be home for the birth of the baby. I was in my eighth month of pregnancy and everything was fine.

The morning dawned a crisp and glittering day. The motorcade slowly moved through the streets of Dallas, Texas.

The president was hit by a rifle's bullet that came from an open window on the sixth floor of a red brick building that faces Dealey Plaza.

United States President John Fitzgerald Kennedy died at 12:55 p.m. in the Parkland Hospital, Dallas, Texas. The date: November 22, 1963.

Luckily, I did not have the television or radio on. I opened the door to see my elderly neighbors Mr. and Mrs. Bartos, standing there.

As I had a smile on my face, they were sure I had not heard the news.

"We want you to come over to our house," they said.

It was not unusual for them to have me over for lunch. They had promised Frank they would keep an eye on me in case the baby decided to come when he was at work.

Once we got inside their house, I knew something was terribly wrong. Mrs. Bartos began to cry and Mr. Bartos had me sit and he brought me a glass of water.

"Is it Frank," I asked, "is Frank okay?"

"No, dear, it's not Frank. It is our President. He has been shot and he died a short time ago.

"We brought you over here because we knew this news would upset you and we are afraid you might go into labor and we can take you to the hospital if you need to go."

I remember asking several times, "You mean President Kennedy? Someone shot President Kennedy?"

Mrs. Bartos and I cried together, while Mr. Bartos nervously kept asking me if I was okay.

I spent the rest of the day with them, going home only after they saw Frank's car pull up in our driveway.

In Frank's arms I felt safe. At this moment, we had each other and our baby was on the way. We grieved for Mrs. Kennedy and her young children. What will happen to them and what is going to happen in our country?

The days ahead were filled with ceremonies; some with grief that touched the soul of our country; some replacing the changing of the guard; revengeful acts as the killer was shot while our nation sought justice.

President Kennedy was killed twenty-six days before our baby was born.

One life left our world; another enters.

Birth and death, the eternal mystery.

Chapter 17

Parent and Duty

"Looking for that tax deduction," Dr. Smith took the solemn look off our faces with his humor.

I am not sure what I was expecting to happen, but I can tell you tax deduction was the furthest thing from my mind.

December 18, 1963, Dr. Smith continued his relaxing and comforting words as he placed our baby in my arms.

"You have a healthy baby boy," he said to Frank and me. Have you chosen a name?"

"Richard," I said, "Richard Victor Perritti."

Leaving the Sanford Memorial Hospital with our baby boy, Frank and I realized we were parents. What did that mean? Okay we knew how we became parents, but how do we be a capable parent?

Forty-five years later, 2008, we still can't answer that question, how do we be a good parent? Sometimes books and instructions can help, but most of the time it is commitment and understanding, bonded with inherent love.

The one thing that Frank and I do know is that our son, Richard, is the pride and joy of our life. We are honored to claim the title, Richard's parents.

Our happiness on Delores Drive was uninterrupted until 1965. Frank received orders for sea duty, Heavy Attack Sqd. 12, NAS Sanford, Weapon Branch LCPO.

These orders meant Frank would be leaving home, going aboard a naval aircraft carrier, performing his military duties during the escalation of the most divisive war in modern United States history.

President Lyndon Johnson, sworn into office following the assassination of President Kennedy, was given the power by Congress to broaden the conflict in the Asian country, Vietnam.

Consumed with the heartache of watching my husband sail away on that ship, I knew there was no time for self-pity. I had a baby to take care of; a home to manage. I had to get used to the feeling of being alone; go on with my normal life without being afraid.

Hardly any American was untouched by the war that was escalating in Vietnam. The media filled the news with reports of domestic dissent and body counts of our dead soldiers.

Kneeling beside our baby's crib, I reached through the slats resting my hand on his small back. As I gently patted, Richard called for his daddy. Frank had always been the one to get him to sleep by patting him on the back. Mother's hand would not do!

His cry growing louder, I tried to explain that Daddy had to go away. I never felt more helpless in my life. Unable to comfort my child, I sat on the floor beside his crib, tears running down my face. In a few moments it was a tiny hand reaching out, gently patting me on the shoulder, which would comfort us both.

"Don't cry, Mommy," he said. "I'll stop if you will," I replied.

Not sure who went to sleep first, but I do know at that time, I realized this getting along without Frank home was going to be a partnership. Throughout all the military years, this never changed.

We would treasure each day that Frank was home with us; we would read his letters over and over when he was away; always praying for his safe return and forever proud of his military service.

Being a military family, we possessed that unique perspective and passion that guide all who serve and protect our country.

The year was 1965 – no cell phones, no e-mail, no fax – all added up to little or no contact.

Once during a nine-month duty out to sea, a ham radio operator in Sanford, Florida patched me through to talk to Frank aboard the ship that was headed for the Mediterranean Sea.

Frank and I would number the outside of our letters because sometimes we would receive four or five at the same time. So, by number we knew which one to open first.

To the military wives of today, I say count your blessings now in the land of the video world. Richard had only a framed photo of his dad that he kept on his night stand and showed it to anyone who came for a visit.

Military wives of today often ask me how I went from being solo parent and household manager when Frank was away to sharing these duties when he was home. My memory goes back to after nine months out at sea, my husband held me in his arms and all I could say was, "Now that you are home do I get the same amount of money? Can I keep the car everyday? Who locks the door at night?"

We laughed!

My only comment is "I was warned!"

Lt. Frank Victor Perritti – United States Navy

Chapter 18

On the Move

There is no greater pride in being a military wife than when your husband is promoted to a higher rank. Standing beside my husband, February 1, 1967, I shared the honor. Frank became a commissioned officer.

After seven promotions during eleven years enlisted, Frank would now wear the uniform of a United States naval officer.

This promotion had a huge impact on Frank's career and our family life. First came the order to report to Naval Air Station, Pensacola, Florida for officer training. Then to NATTC, Jacksonville, Florida.

We were on the move. After selling our first home together, I moved into an apartment near Orlando. This was to be a holding station until Frank's training was complete. Missing his son and his wife, Frank moved us into an apartment in Pensacola, then a hotel room in Jacksonville.

In both places I was surrounded by other military families and it was kind of fun living gypsy-like. The best part, we were together.

Frank and Father Antos's words began to ring true. After the, "will you be my wife and share my life," came you will have no control over when or where you live and you must be able to pack and unpack quickly.

Was I ready to embrace this topsy-turvy life on a long-term basis? As far as I was concerned, at this point, I had no choice. My son needed me, my husband needed me; all the challenges would be surmountable as long as we were together.

Getting to know other military wives during our stay in Pensacola and Jacksonville, I realized even if we did share so many common bonds, no two wives are the same.

Sacrifices had to be made. How we handled them would determine our happiness.

In time I came to understand that wherever a military wife lives on history's timeline, she must possess enduring courage, ageless resilience and an impenetrable spirit for her country and her family.

From the beginning I could see the light at the end of the tunnel. With determination, I was not going to allow my sacrifices to be a lonely reminder of my life as a military wife.

FACTS

Date I became a military wife

Marriage: Martha Lou Killgore - Frank Victor Perritti
March 17, 1962, Sanford Naval Air Station, Sanford, Florida

John Fitzgerald Kennedy: (1917-1963)

United States President 1961-1963. He was the youngest elected president at that time. Supporter of the U.S. Space Program to put a man on the moon; established the Peace Corps; favored government programs for the elderly and education. His greatest challenge as President, the Cuban Missile Crisis. President Kennedy was assassinated on November 22, 1963, in Dallas, Texas, by Lee Harvey Oswald.

Cuban Missile Crisis: October 22, 1962

I found myself scared and afraid, knowing my husband was aboard the aircraft carrier *Independence* underway to set up a naval blockade of Cuba, under orders of President Kennedy. President Kennedy received Air Force photographs showing Soviet Union missile launch sites in Cuba. The nuclear missiles could reach and destroy many U.S. cities.

President Kennedy demanded that the Soviet Union remove the missiles. On October 24, Soviet Premier Nikita Khrushchev angrily threatened to fight what he called an "act of piracy" by the United States. During the days that passed, the United States made plans to invade Cuba. The world braced for nuclear war.

October 28, Khrushchev agreed to remove the missiles and destroy the launch sites.

The crisis was over.

Death of a President: November 22, 1963

John Fitzgerald Kennedy, 35th president of the United States, was assassinated.

On a political trip to Dallas, Texas, President Kennedy's presidential limousine had the bulletproof top down because the weather was beautiful; no need to shield him from the elements. The twenty-four car motorcade moved through Dallas. It rolled slowly allowing time for the Kennedys to wave from the back of the limousine.

Passing through downtown, they turned right and then sharply left, slowing as they entered a park called Dealey Plaza.

Above and behind the motorcade, from an open window on the sixth floor of a red brick building, the air cracked as a rifle bullet zipped toward the limousine. It hit the president in the upper back, exited through his throat, and traveled on, wounding Governor John Connally, who was in the front seat. Another bullet found the right rear quadrant of the president's head.

A quote by Jacqueline Kennedy, President Kennedy's wife, *"I was looking....to the left, and I heard these terrible noises... And my husband never made a sound. So I turned to the right, and all I remember is seeing my husband, he had this sort of quizzical look on his face, and his hand was up."*

President Kennedy slumped against his wife as his limousine roared toward nearby Parkland Hospital. 12:55 p.m., November 22, 1963, John Fitzgerald Kennedy died.

The world subsequently changed.

President Lyndon B. Johnson: (1908-1973)

Sworn into office as president of the United States when President Kennedy was assassinated. Term of office: 1963-1969.

While in office he established several social programs that improved conditions for the poor and the elderly.

In 1965, he sent U.S. troops to fight the Vietnam War.

Richard Victor Perritti

Born, December 18, 1963, Sanford, Florida. He maintains a success-ful career in government administration.

Education: Lyman High School, Longwood, Florida; Seminole Junior College, Lake Mary, Florida; Technical College of the Air Force; Oklahoma Central State, Edmond, Oklahoma; master's degree, Florida State University, Tallahassee, Florida.

Work: Jacobson's Department Store, Father's lawn business; United States Air Force; City of Hollywood, Florida; Lee County, Fort Myers, Florida; State of Florida, Tallahassee, Florida.

2008, he is on the staff of the governor of Florida.

Most important position – My son

Vietnam War:

Never declared a war with the United States. 1965, President Johnson sent U.S. troops into South Vietnam to help stop communist aggression by the North Vietnamese.

1969, end of President Johnson's term in office, there were 540,000 U.S. troops in Vietnam.

1973, a cease-fire was signed; U.S. troops were withdrawn, under the direction of U.S. President Richard Nixon. More that 57,000 Americans died or remain missing in Vietnam.

April 30, 1975, South Vietnam surrendered to the communists.

Anti-war sentiments in the United States remain to this day. In Washington, D.C. there stands a Vietnam War Memorial, inscribed with the names of the more than 57,000 Americans who died or remain missing in Vietnam.

This war caused a great deal of conflict in the United States.

February 1, 1967: Frank Victor Perritti, Jr., commissioned as officer in the United States Navy.

March 1967 – May 1967: Orders to Naval Air Station, Pensacola, Florida.

May 1967 – June 1967: Orders to NATTC, Jacksonville, Florida.

Cold War: As evident by the Cuban Missile Crisis, the threat of nuclear annihilation prevailed between the United States and the Soviet Union. It was the explosion of an atomic bomb in 1945 that inaugurated the nuclear age.

There would be four decades of truculent cold war rhetoric between the United States and the Soviet Union.

Times of Turmoil in the United States: 1969-1974

Richard Milhous Nixon was the 37th President of the United States. Unfortunately, he will be remembered as the first president to resign from office. Because of his involvement in illegal campaign activities, called the Watergate scandal, Congress proceeded to remove him from office.

Before this time, Richard Nixon had dedicated his life to the service of the United States. After World War II service in the Navy, Nixon served in Congress from 1947 to 1952. There he won a reputation of pursuing charges of communist subversion in government. He was elected vice president in 1952 and 1956 as running mate to Dwight D. Eisenhower, the Republican candidate. In 1960, Nixon narrowly lost the presidential election to John F. Kennedy. In another close race, against Democrat Hubert Humphrey, he was elected president in 1968.

Nixon ended United States participation in the Vietnam War and improved relations with the Soviet Union and China.

In 1973, under Nixon's leadership, a settlement was reached resulting in the withdrawal of all American forces from Vietnam.

In 1972, Nixon visited China and began a process that later resulted in diplomatic ties with the communist regime there. He was the first U.S. president to visit China.

In 1972, Nixon visited the Soviet Union and signed an agreement to limit nuclear weapons.

Nixon was re-elected by a landslide in 1972.

The Vietnam War - Not only during the years of involvement in this war, but remaining to date a great deal of conflict in the nation. Pro- and anti-war sentiments part of the United States culture.

History in order to know how this happened—southeast Asia, country of Vietnam was part of a colony known as French Indochina from the 1860s until World War II, when the Japanese took control.

After the war, France took control again, but the Vietnamese people began to fight for their independence. The French were defeated and forced to pull out in 1954. They left the country divided. North Vietnam was a communist country supported by China and the Soviet Union. South Vietnam looked to the West for support.

Beginning in 1957, North Vietnam gave aid to South Vietnamese communists called Viet Cong. They tried to overthrow the South Vietnamese government. The United States, which wanted to stop communist aggression, began to aid South Vietnam. Troops were sent beginning in 1965. By 1969, at the end of Lyndon Johnson's term as president, there were 540,000 U.S. troops in Vietnam. After Richard Nixon became president in 1969, he began to withdraw U.S. troops. In 1973, a cease-fire was signed, and U.S. troops were withdrawn. But in 1975, the Communists mounted a strong offensive, and South Vietnam was forced to surrender on April 30, 1975. The neighboring countries of Laos and Cambodia also fell to the Communists. Vietnam was reunited under communist rule in 1976.

Chapter 19

Landing in Puerto Rico

For five years I had been on my home turf with family; now I was going to be a "real military wife."

Boarding a plane in Miami, Florida, Richard and I were on our way to join Frank at his new duty station: Naval Air Station, Roosevelt Roads, Puerto Rico.

In later years, Frank was surprised to learn that this was probably the happiest time in my life. I had no sadness when leaving the U.S. mainland; so ready to embrace a new land, new people, new way of living.

Landing at the San Juan airport, I was immediately introduced to the "new" people. I couldn't understand a word they were saying, although I had taken Spanish language in school. This was not going to be easy.

Richard and I were happy to see Frank in the crowd and we were so wondrously surprised when we arrived at our new home on the military base, Roosevelt Roads.

The driveway sloped downward to a white stucco house, built during World War II. Seemingly the house was planted on a hillside and embedded in a lush foliage landscape. I couldn't believe my eyes as I gazed across the lawn to see beautiful blues and greens of water with an island on the far horizon.

The island was St. Thomas and, no, I wasn't dreaming. So far, where was the down side to our first military transfer away from our childhood home?

Friends became family as I was introduced to the elite network of military wives. I learned that socializing was an important role in being the wife of naval officer.

Many events were social obligations, although, how you responded was personal choice. Frank and I enjoyed the Officer's Bowling League, attending the base chapel, hail and farewell parties and parties at the Officer's Club. I became the president of the Ladies Officers' Wives Bowling League and a year later, became the president of the Officers' Wives Club.

I could easily write a book on my experiences while president of the Officers' Wives Club, 1969-1970. Highlights were: being honored by my peers in electing me to be their president; attending meetings with the high ranking officers responsible for our naval base operations; in charge of luncheons where our guests were different U.S. Senator's wives and other dignitaries; in a position to organize charitable events for purposes of things like; putting air conditioning in the enlisted service man's section of the naval base hospital; also, providing supplies to people in need who lived on nearby islands and Puerto Rico.

I accepted my presidency as an honor to my country and service of the military wives. It was a year of learning how the inside path of military leadership works; always beginning and ending in Washington, D.C.

I believe my greatest accomplishment was leaving the club a written constitution that would provide a structure for this permanent organization.

Dear to my heart are all the military wives who stood with me during the good times and the bad times. Yes, I said bad times. As with most organizations, there are times when decisions have to be made and there is no pleasing everyone. The difficulty in the military is when the husband of the military wife you are trying to accommodate, when her husband outranks your husband. Sometimes he is your husband's boss!

My decisions were always based on doing the right thing and what was legal. At the end of my term, the highest ranking officer's wife, Mrs. Johns, gave a luncheon in my honor. Officers' wives of all ranks, from highest to lowest, attended and I felt privileged to call each one of these ladies my friend.

When I asked my friend Harriett, "How do I pay you for everything you do for me and for always taking care of Richard on occasions when Frank and I can't take him with us?"

Harriett's reply, "Pass it on. Everything I do for you, you do for someone else."

I never forgot those words and I spent the rest of our military years doing just that. These early friendships were golden. Although the time came when we walked away from each other, years passed and years later we would see each other and it was as though we were never apart.

This was so true with my friend Kay. Kay's husband was a military doctor and they had a young girl named Sheila. Later they were blessed with two boys, Sean and Steve.

Living next door to each other, we formed a bonding family relationship that has never been broken. Richard refers to Sheila as his sister. The taking care of each other began on this island called Puerto Rico and the taking care of each other has not ended.

Where, When, Why

June 1967- Puerto Rico

♦ Military Orders June 1967 – June 1970

♦ Naval Air Station, Roosevelt Roads, Puerto Rico

♦ Weapons Department

Puerto Rico

♦ A tropical island with consistent easterly trade winds. A place of sunny beaches, upland rain forests and urban highways that intersect with country roads.

♦ This Caribbean island of enchantment is located between the Caribbean Sea and the North Atlantic Ocean; (1,600 km) southeast of Miami, Florida.

♦ The island's maximum length is 180 km (110 mi.); width 65 km (40 mi.)

♦ November 19, 1493, Christopher Columbus discovered the island during his second voyage to the New World.

♦ The Taino Indians, who came from South America, were found inhabiting the island. The first Spanish settlement was not built there until 1508. It remained a Spanish colony until 1898, when the United States took control following the Spanish-American War.

♦ Originally the Spanish called the island San Juan Bautista, for St. John the Baptist and the town Puerto Rico because of its obvious excellent potentialities. Later the two names were switched. San Juan became the capital city of Puerto Rico, a commonwealth of the United States.

♦ The president of the United States is the chief of state; the head of the island's government is an elected governor.

♦ The Puerto Rican people continue to debate the status of their homeland. Many want Puerto Rico to remain a commonwealth associated with the United States. Others want it to become the 51st state. And others want it to become independent.

♦ There are seventy eight municipalities recognized in Puerto Rico of which each has a mayor. In one of these municipalities is the town of Ceiba, located in the eastern part of Puerto Rico. Near this town and the town called Fajardo, the United States Government built the Roosevelt Roads Naval Base.

Roosevelt Roads Naval Base – 1919 Assistant Secretary of the Navy, Franklin D. Roosevelt, on a surveying trip, conceived the idea of building a naval base on the eastern part of Puerto Rico.

- Named for its founder, the base would eventually become one of the largest naval facilities in the world. The base encompassed more than 100 miles of paved roads, more than 30 tenant commands and 1,300 buildings, homes to 7,000 personnel.
- 1943- First commissioned as a U.S. Naval Operations Base. The keystone of the Caribbean Defense System. This base was a well-protected anchorage, a major air station and an industrial establishment capable of supporting 60 percent of the Atlantic fleet under wartime conditions. There were rumors that if the British Empire ever fell to Axis powers, Roosevelt Roads would become their new operating base for the British fleet.
- 1943 – With Allied operations focusing on Europe and the Pacific, the major defense hub on the island was unnecessary.
- 1944 – Naval operating base was put in maintenance status.
- 1957 – The base becomes a major training site for U.S. fleet exercises.
- 1941 – During World War II, the United States military purchased about two-thirds of the island called Vieques. This area became an extension of the Roosevelt Road Military Base and was used for a testing ground for over 60 years.

Vieques Island

- ◆ Taino Indians' word for small island (beigues). Caribbean Island, 21 miles long and 3 miles wide; located between Puerto Rico and St. Thomas. Only 8 miles of sea separates it from the Roosevelt Roads Naval Base on the Puerto Rico mainland.

- ◆ 1493 – Not sure if Christopher Columbus went to Vieques, but during the early 16th century the island was claimed by Spain. For 300 years it was a lawless outpost, frequented by pirates and outlaws. It was not a permanent colony, but the Spanish did govern and annexed it to Puerto Rico.

- ◆ 1898 – When the mainland of Puerto Rico was ceded by Spain to the United States, Vieques was included.

Memories of Vieques

I remember this island in the sun with its pristine, deserted beaches. It was important to Frank, Richard, and me because as the Weapons Officer of Roosevelt Roads, one of Frank's duties was being in charge of naval operations on Vieques.

When possible, Richard and I would ride the ferry over to the island to be with Frank. Eating in the mess tent, sleeping on a cot, no ladies' bath available; made me appreciate my house on the mainland.

I learned to appreciate our naval personnel and the sacrifices they make. The problems of the military wives pale in comparison.

On quiet days, I walked alone on the white sandy beach, stopping to pick up a shell or two. I remember my meditation filled with emotion of loneliness, almost lost in this glorious world that God created.

My trance was interrupted by Richard's laughter coming from the jeep down the beach. "Mom," he yelled, "Come get in, Dad is waiting down at the ferry. We have to leave."

The navy man greeted me as I climbed aboard the jeep. I thanked the driver for riding Richard around with him in the jeep, as it was apparent the jeep riding was Richard's favorite thing to do on Vieques Island.

The driver left us at the landing to wait for the ferry. Richard was playing, throwing pebbles into the water when he called out, "Daddy, look, there is a little fish out of the water."

Poor little fish was flopping around on the boat ramp. Frank, being the good daddy for his son, proceeded to give the fish a little kick back into the water. The problem was it wasn't only the fish that went into the water. Frank slipped and in an instant he disappeared.

No ferry in sight, just Richard and I on the pier, no need to yell for help, no one could hear. The water was black, deep, I can't swim, Richard and I hold onto each other. I screamed over and over, "Frank, Frank!"

"Mom, is Daddy coming back?" Richard asked over and over.

It seemed to take forever, then a miracle – up popped Frank's head. He struggled to pull himself up the slippery ramp. To this day, he can't explain how he got out of there.

No dry clothes to change in, he boarded the ferry wearing his wet uniform, missing his hat.

"What happened, Sir?" the ferry boat captain asked.

"I went for a swim with the fishes," Frank laughed.

How close Richard and I came to not remembering Vieques as the beautiful island in the sun, but where we lost Frank. Not as a military naval officer doing his job, but the culprit was a "little fish."

On May 2003, the U.S. Navy withdrew from Vieques and much of the island was designated a wildlife reserve under the control of the U.S. Fish and Wildlife Service.

On September 30, 2003, the president of the United States signed into law the Fiscal Year 2004 Defense Appropriation Act. The legislation included language that called for the Navy to close Naval Station Roosevelt Roads.

2004, the Navy relocated U.S. Naval Forces Southern Command from Naval Station Roosevelt Roads, Puerto Rico to Naval Station Mayport, Florida.

Roosevelt Roads Officers' Wives Club

♦ U.S. Naval Station

♦ Roosevelt Roads

♦ Puerto Rico

♦ Constitution adopted by a majority of the active membership at the February 14, 1970 meeting of the Roosevelt Roads Officers' Wives Club. Signed by Martha Perritti, President.

Nothings Perfect – No Place Is Without Crime - Unfortunately, we remember the bad days as well as the good ones.

The morning began a wonderful sunny day. Frank, Richard and I decided to go shopping in San Juan. Arriving at a gardening shop, Frank pulled the car in the back parking lot. Frank began to pick out some stepping stones for his landscaping project, as Richard and I walked into the back of the shop. Richard pulled loose of my hand and for a few seconds I focused on several books that were on display.

Feeling Richard missing from my side, I looked to the other side of the counter; I didn't see him. My eyes surveyed the shop. Terror struck me; a man had Richard in his arms, carrying him out the front door to the street.

My memory fades, but my screams alerted Frank and the shop keeper. They both ran into the street. In heavy traffic, the man sat

Richard down and escaped in his car that was parked across the street from the shop.

Frank picked Richard up and brought him safely to me. The shop keeper was cursing at the kidnapper and apologizing to us.

"Please, please," he said, "don't bring the baby when you come shopping in San Juan. The kidnappers see you are American and they take the children for money."

It was a painful lesson to learn. Now, at age forty-four, Richard is reminded he could have grown up in the sugar cane fields of Puerto Rico. Makes him appreciate the life he has had.

Kidnapping is an element of crime that happens throughout the world, not only in San Juan, Puerto Rico.

U.S.S. Independence (referenced in chapter 15).

Chapter 20

From Sunshine to Gray Skies

So clear is my memory of standing in the hallway of the Roosevelt Roads Elementary School not knowing what to do next.

"Mrs. Perritti, you can go home now. The bus driver will bring Richard home when school is out," said the school principal.

Could it be that our baby boy, Richard, was old enough to be in kindergarten? I believe that was the longest day of my life, as I realized this was the beginning of my son's independence. I had many questions about his educational journey and fears for his future.

I would like to tell you that these days of new school beginnings and all the parent emotions that go with it became easier as the years passed, but to be truthful that "lost" feeling I had on that first day of elementary school, remains to this day. I have learned to replace the fear with faith, trust and belief in Richard's judgment.

Reading his resume, anyone would be impressed with his scholarly accomplishments; his experience and strength of character.

As years go by, beginnings are placed in our past and their importance is overlooked. In the military, little time is allowed to dwell on what is happening in the present and rapidly events become history.

One day, we are living on an island, soaking up the sun, blessed with friendships, Frank's naval career providing all necessary for our family life. Strange how one sheet of paper can change all that. Not so strange when you read the top of the page – SEA DUTY.

I never met a man in the navy who actually wanted to go to sea!

The expression on Frank's face showed concern as he read me the orders:

> "Report for Sea Duty aboard the
> USS Wasp, CVA-18,
> Homeport, Quonset Point
> Naval Air Station, Rhode Island."

Here comes the downside of being a military family. From three years of living in the sunshine of the beautiful Puerto Rican island to the gray skies and gray ship of Quonset Point, Rhode Island.

Having grown up in the south, Alabama and Florida, the only thing I knew about Rhode Island was what I had learned in school. Basically it was our smallest state, called a New England state and it snowed there. I had seen snow only a couple of times. As a small child I saw it in Alabama and once in high school, 1958, in Florida. I recall the school bell ringing and the announcer on the audio system instructed everyone to go outside, as snowflakes were falling! There was intense excitement over a few snowflakes.

Promising my son many things in order to soften the hardship of moving; we assured him he would be able to play in the snow.

That promise may seem silly to others, but military parents search for the positives when reasoning with children in accepting the challenges of adjusting to new home, new school, new friends.

The bottom line it is "Daddy's job." As military wives, we encourage our children to be understanding and supportive of Daddy's job. Be proud of the fact he not only provides for his family, he takes care of our entire country. The military family must share that responsibility.

The white curtains had been carefully packed; ready to hang in our next available housing. All our belongings were gone. Only a few suitcases remained with necessities for our brief visit with our families in Florida.

My memory is so clear – knocking on Kay's door, her answering, "Come in." She sat in a chair. She was wearing the adorable maternity dress she had made.

Soon she would have her third child. I would not see Steve until he was a teenager. Sheila stood by her mother's side and Sean was in his crib, playing.

Kay barely looked up as she said, "I want to thank you, Martha, for always helping me take care of the children. You have been such a good friend."

I hugged her good-bye, gave Sheila and Sean a hug. I don't remember leaving them there. That was the memory I didn't keep.

This was a lasting friendship, not uncommon among military wives of all time.

The island grew smaller as the plane soared over the blue waters. "Mommy, are you crying?" Richard asked. "I will be all right," I assured him.

Frank turned from his seat in front of us. "Everything will be fine, Richard," he assured us both.

We trusted him; everything would be fine. We were together.

Chapter 21

Quonset Point

Our being together would not last long. At the time, there was no allowance for emotion. We had to focus on the task at hand.

Where was this place called Quonset Point, Rhode Island and what was this thing called USS Wasp – CVS-18?

After a brief visit with family in Florida, we drove to Rhode Island. Greeted by our good friends Dick, his wife, Letta, their two children and Boco, the poodle; we were invited to stay with them until we got a place of our own. In fact, Dick was leaving to serve on the USS Intrepid and Letta was taking the two children on a trip. Boco would stay home with Richard and me.

Watching his dad board a plane, Richard asked, "Mom, where is the ship?"

"It's far away," I explained, "He has to go on the plane to meet the ship."

Richard was silent as we drove away from the airport. I was afraid.

First, I had to find my way to Dick and Letta's house, next I had to find a place for Richard and me to live once Letta returned.

So many times I could hear the words of warning from Father Antos: "Many times you will be on your own. When duty calls for Frank to leave, he must go."

Luckily, Letta's next-door neighbor put their small house up for rent. Richard and I were excited. We had friends in the neighborhood and school was only a block away and, best of all, we had our own place. Everything was prepared for when Daddy would come home.

Watching this monster of a ship slowly maneuver its way to the Quonset Point dock; feeling the pride and joy of my country and my husband, I hugged my son and whispered through the tears "Frank's home."

Richard asked, "Mom, is that the ship Daddy is on?"

"Yes, son, that is the USS Wasp – CVS-18."

Men in white uniforms lined the flight deck of the shadow-gray ship; the crowd on the pier cheered their happiness; military families would be united, if only for a short time.

Frank, Richard and I treasured each day we were together. We enjoyed picnics in the park; trips to the wonderful land of Nova Scotia; and the changing seasons in the woods of Vermont.

Life was better than normal, so much so that I forgot the number one rule for a military family – **Be Flexible**.

Easy to follow this rule when we were in Puerto Rico where I was involved in many aspects of life on the military base. I had perspective and passion for making a difference in people's lives.

Standing on the pier at Quonset Point, Richard and I held onto each other as we waved goodbye to the USS Wasp-CVS-18, pulling out to sea.

It was like darkness and I couldn't find the **Flexible** button.

At night when I closed the door to our rented house; tucked my son into bed; took out paper and pen to write Frank a letter; I was alone.

Difficult time to recognize the overall scheme and the role our military family played in it. Although I had a clear understanding of our commitment and I was fully aware of the high level of tangible and intangible support provided by the military, I suffered from depression. Depression so severe that at one point I was hospitalized.

This was the roughest time for me during my lifetime. I don't want to dwell on this time; so therefore, I will focus on my recovery.

First of all, my loving husband took charge to make sure I had good medical care and a happy home. When he had to go aboard the ship, he had his sister come and stay with Richard and me.

I will always be grateful to Frank's sister and many military friends who cared for me every step of the way.

Coping with depression is probably the worst affliction for military wives. Believe me, if I can suffer from it, it is a tough nut to crack.

SOCIAL REGISTER

USS WASP

USS WASP (CVS-18)

AUGUST 1970

Chapter 22

USS WASP-CVS-18 Decommissioned

The United States government made the decision to decommission the USS WASP – CVS-18. This meant the ship would be taken out of service in the United States Naval Fleet.

Bad news came after the ship pulled into the Newport News, Virginia shipyard. The navy was hoping repairs could be made and the WASP would once again join the ("Mothball") Atlantic Reserve Fleet as it did on February 17, 1947.

Problems too major and repairs too costly; the USS WASP returned to Quonset Point where preparations were made for decommissioning.

Crew members, whether past or present, are always affected when their ship is decommissioned.

Frank recalls his service aboard the USS WASP – CVS-18.

"I served this historical ship, June 1970-July 1972. I was the last officer in charge of Ordnance Handling to serve on the USS WASP.

Operations included sea duty in the Mediterranean Sea, the South Atlantic and Caribbean, and the North Atlantic. Tracking a Russian submarine was said to be impossible. The ship and crew did the impossible at that time and earned a United States President Citation. That was the last citation given to the USS WASP-CVS-18.

Most of the ship's crew transferred progressively. I was one of the last to leave.

Pulling away from the pier, I looked into my rear view mirror, 1 July 1972; the United States flag had been removed.

The rest of my military career I would have the honorary title – "Air Gunner."

I am sorry to say, at the time I did not appreciate the importance of Frank's career. It had been a rough time for me these past two years.

One of the happiest days of my life was when Frank walked in the door and asked, "Where do you want to go, Chicago or Sicily?"

"Sicily," was my answer without any hesitation.

"Are you sure?" Frank looked puzzled.

"Positive, positive," I repeated.

"Okay," he said, "Sicily it is."

"Richard," he says, "my son, we are going to live in Sicily."

Changing his clothes out of his navy uniform, Frank followed Richard and our dog, Bingo – father, son, dog, it was play time.

It was time for me to prepare dinner. Washing my hands at the kitchen sink, I gazed out the window, "Where in the world is Sicily?"

Rhode Island

♦ In the year 1524, King Francis I of France sent Giovanni da Verrazano to find a short route to China. Verrazano was born in Italy, but had joined the French navy. Sailing west he explored the Narragansett bays on the coast of the new world. His discoveries were considered a failure because none of them led to the Far East.

♦ In the year 1492, Christopher Columbus, an Italian, sailed for the Spanish King Ferdinand and Queen Isabella. He too was searching for a route to Asia and he believed he had found it when he landed on islands in the Caribbean. His voyages did open up the settlement of the Western Hemisphere.

♦ An Italian navigator and explorer, Amerigo Vespucci was convinced that this land he and Columbus discovered was not Asia. In 1507, a German mapmaker named Martin Waldseemuller made a map of the area that Vespucci had explored and named the area America.

♦ Colonies began to form into what became the United States of America. In 1636, Roger Williams had been expelled from the colony of Massachusetts for promoting religious and political freedom.

♦ Williams founded the state of Rhode Island, located on Narragansett Bay. One of the thirteen original New England states, Rhode Island's statehood was declared May 29, 1790. Today it remains the smallest state in the union.

Quonset Point Naval Air Station – An incredible tapestry of events propelled the association between the United States Navy and Rhode Island.

♦ Several hundred years have passed since: John Paul Jones (1747-1792), a great naval hero of the American Revolution, was called the "father of the United States Navy"; Americans prevailed over the

British on their invasion of Rhode Island in 1778 and Quonset Point Naval Air Station was located along side the home of the Seabees, the naval base at Davisville.

♦ After the year 1884, several important naval schools were established in this area.

♦ The Naval War College blossomed during the second half of the 19th century. Then in the first half of the 20th century the naval presence in Narragansett Bay had a huge influx of military personnel because of World War I and World War II.

♦ Three presidents of the United States attended the naval schools in this area:

♦ John F. Kennedy – trained in PT boat operations in the fall of 1942.

♦ Richard M. Nixon – basic officer training 1942. Two months at Quonset Point Naval Air Station, across the Narragansett Bay from Newport, Rhode Island.

♦ George H. W. Bush, flight training at Charlestown, south of Quonset Point. Lt. Bush proposed to his wife, Barbara, while he was stationed there.

♦ It is doubtful the three men ever met face to face during their time here; but, when you consider how small Rhode Island is, it's not unreasonable to think that their paths may have crossed at one time or the other.

♦ Between 1945 and 1973, the U.S. Navy was Rhode Island's largest civilian employer. This ended in 1973 when the federal government decided to relocate many ships.

♦ The elite schools for the U.S. Navy remain.

♦ **Trivia Fact:** Quonset Hut – trademark for a prefabricated shelter made of corrugated metal, shaped like a long half of a cylinder, resting on its flat surface.

♦ The Quonset Hut was named after Quonset Point, Rhode Island, where it was first manufactured.

History of the Ninth U.S.S. WASP

♦ The keel of aircraft carrier, CV-18, Quincy, Massachusetts. She was commissioned U.S.S. WASP CV-18 on November 24, 1943. She was the ninth navy ship to bear the WASP name.

♦ She served gallantly during World War II. After the war the WASP was given a rest. She was decommissioned and attached to the Atlantic Reserve Fleet.

♦ The call to join the awakening "Jet Age" came in the early 1950s. The WASP was removed from the reserve fleet and ordered to the New York Naval Shipyard for alterations so she could accommodate large, heavier and faster aircraft.

♦ She was recommissioned and designated an attack carrier, CVA-18. The conversion from the old straight flight deck to the more useful angled deck was completed in December 1955. November 1, 1956, the Wasp was designated an anti-submarine carrier, CVA-18.

♦ Operations were continuous in the South Atlantic, Caribbean and Mediterranean seas.

♦ The crew of the WASP named her the "Mighty Stinger". The Mighty Stinger gained fame as an agent for peace by recovering five pairs of Gemini astronauts (Gemini IV, VI, VII, IX, and XII).

♦ This great American naval fighting ship was decommissioned July 1, 1972.

♦ A decommissioning coin was given to the last crew that served the
USS WASP. The engraved lettering reads:

"In commemoration of the Officers and Crew

who served aboard the Aircraft Carrier

USS WASP (CVS-18) during her twenty-nine

years of faithful service to her country

on her decommissioning on July 1, 1972

at Quonset Point, Rhode Island."

USS WASP

1943   CV-18, CVA-18, CVS018   1972

"Air Gunner" – An honorary title given to officers in charge of
ordnance handling.   Frank Perritti was the last officer in charge of
ordnance handling to serve on the USS WASP – CVS-18.

Other ships he served on:

USS Independence – CVA – 62

USS Saratoga – CVA – 60

USS WASP – CVS – 18

Bingo – In Providence, Rhode Island, September 10, 1970 this silky
terrier was born.   Wee Tiny Tim his breeder called him.   Frank decided
to get a dog for Richard because Dad had to be away so much on sea
duty.   Looking in the Sunday newspaper he noticed a breeder's ad for
silky terriers.

No time was wasted going to the breeder's house.   The room
was crowded with puppies.   Each one was fighting for an eating
position.   While Frank and I talked to the breeder, Richard observed the
situation.   He reached down to the outside of the crowded litter and
picked up this tiny, black and tan puppy.

"Mom," he said, "We need to take this one. He is hungry and the other puppies won't let him eat."

"Oh, that is Tiny Tim. I am not sure he will make it, him being so little," the breeder explained.

Richard held the tiny pup closer. "Dad, can we take him home with us?"

So it was, the three of us drove home with Richard holding Tiny Tim.

"Mom, can we give him a new name? After we feed him, he won't be tiny anymore and the name Tiny Tim won't be good for him."

Names were discussed among the three of us and the decision was made. Bingo is his name.

The tiny puppy now had a home of his own; a bed, plenty of food, water and an abundance of love.

For several weeks he remained shy and bashful, then one evening during our after dinner walk, the transformation happened. All of a sudden Bingo stopped, gave his body a good shake, reared back his shoulders and began to strut. His change in demeanor was so profound, that we have never forgotten this walk with Bingo.

Richard says, "It's the day Bingo became a Perritti."

We were blessed to have him in our family for ten years. Our military life was not always easy for him. There was a lot of traveling by car and airline flights to foreign lands. He was a real trooper and our one constant joy.

Not until Frank retired from the military did Bingo leave us. Our memories are often shared. Tiny Tim, our Bingo, will never be forgotten.

Chapter 23

Passport to a Foreign Land

1972, sea duty had ended. New military orders read:

"Report to duty station, United States Air Facility (USNAF), Sigonella, Sicily.
Two-year overseas shore duty with dependents."

For my husband it was his job as he prepared for his new duty station. For our son, Richard, and me, it was our passport to a foreign land.

I will admit, after checking the world map, I was a little nervous; but, the decision had been made, "Sicily here we come!"

Medical records were pulled at the Quonset Point base hospital and we had to have a complete physical and several medical shots. Even Bingo, our silky terrier, had to be inoculated for the journey and our life in Sicily.

Today as I look at my photo of the passport, April 7, 1972, besides looking young, I can recognize the apprehension in my face. Maybe I am just remembering my feelings.

One thing I am sure of I was not unhappy about leaving Quonset Point. I try to remember only the good times during our stay at Quonset Point, but the effects of depression lingered for years.

I do realize I am not alone; as military wives, we know there are others who suppress the anxiety of depression returning. It is a common ground we each have to deal with in our own way.

Leaving Quonset Point, we headed south for a visit with my parents before we departed on our new adventure.

Frank traveled to Sicily before Richard and me. He reported for duty, secured a house for us to live in and prepared provisions for our arrival.

Bingo was next to make the trip from Florida USA to Sicily. He arrived in good shape, so everything was coming together as planned.

Leaving the arms of my parents was not as easy as it had been five years before.

Puerto Rico was only a couple of hours away by flight from Florida. This time my destination was a couple of days by flight and an ocean would separate us. I worried about never seeing my father again. He was eighty four years old.

Traveling to this land called Sicily was not an easy thing to do, but Richard and I took everything in stride. After all, we knew Frank was there waiting for us and Bingo would be by his side.

I calmed my apprehensions by believing the fact that we had lived three wonderful years in Puerto Rico, which is an island. Looking at the world map, I saw Sicily is an island. So how bad could it be?

Richard and I settled in for our long flight from New York to Rome, Italy. Raising the window shade on the 747, seeing the sun rise over the snow-covered French Alps; I had never seen anything so spectacular.

That was only the beginning to three years of my life filled with sights, sounds and experiences of living in a foreign land.

"Look, Richard, look," the only words that could come from me as the plane circled revealing the magnificent view of Mt. Etna.

The Allitalia pilots invited Richard into the cockpit where he was more interested in the plane than the view out the window.

Stepping off the plane in Catania, Sicily; letting go of Richard's hand as he ran into his dad's arms; I was a stranger in this land; a fleeting thought. Only feelings of happiness when this man in his United States naval officer's uniform kissed me. Frank, Richard, Bingo, and I were together; that's all that mattered.

Sicily

Sicily is the largest of the Italian islands, has a triangular shape (from which it perhaps derives its ancient name of Trinacria), measuring 160 miles in length and varying in width from 30 miles at its western end to about 110 miles in the east. Sicily is separated from the mainland of Italy by the narrow (less than two nautical miles wide) straits of Messina; it is the largest island in the Mediterranean.

Many necropolae and grottoes scattered around the island proves that Sicily was populated in prehistoric times. Because of the island's location in the center of the Mediterranean – midway between Europe and North Africa, the Straits of Gibraltar and the Middle East – Sicily attracted many conquerors.

Sicily has a long and rich history due to the constant occupation by foreign powers.

It is believed the Greeks were the first conquerors to arrive, calling the island "Trinacria." The Romans, Byzantines, Arabs, Normans, Germans, Spaniards, French and Austrians followed, all helping to shape Sicily's past.

Present-day Sicily reflects this rich heritage. Catacombs, Roman amphitheaters, Greek temples and theatres and Arab baths are mixed among the modern cities. Sicilians speak Italian and the Sicilian dialect, a mix of Greek, Latin, Arabic, Spanish, and Italian. The people are very warm, friendly and hospitable, particularly to those interested in learning their way of life and language. They are also very religious and celebrate with many elaborate religious festivals and holidays.

The economy is largely agricultural: the main cultivations are wheat, grapevines, olive trees, vegetables and fruits. A large segment devotes itself to fishing: swordfish, tuna, eels and sardines.

A considerably advanced chemical industry is linked to the mining industry: sulphur, potassium, salts, asphalt and oil.

The roadways are lined with fresh fruit and vegetable stands and in the cities open-air markets offer everything from Italian shoes to household goods.

The island is noted for its fine embroidery, hand-woven cloth carpets and jewelry, made from native coral, which grows offshore. Pottery is a popular item to buy due to its unique design and durability.

Being an island, Sicily is surrounded by beaches ranging from soft white sand to huge lava rocks. The land is mostly mountainous and is characterized by volcanic phenomena, created by the largest volcano in Europe, Mount Etna.

Etna

Etna is the largest of all Europe's active volcanoes. Its conical profile appears in all its splendor. Sides of the mountain reveal a mass of lava streams, superimposed one on the other through the centuries, powerful and black.

Etna's height is always variable (estimation 3300 meters) due to its continued eruptions. During the eruptions it spews great masses of incandescent lava and according to their greater or lesser fluidity and to the steepness of the terrain, it is channeled into enormous streams and torrents of fire, which have often come close to and even destroyed, the villages below.

Frank and Richard traveled to the top, passing close to the most recent lava streams. The lava was still quite hot and they observed small secondary cones that have opened up during recent years.

Looking inside the enormous mouth, one can see the lava boiling at the bottom. Frank describes it as, "looking like bubbling cream of wheat."

From the moment I first saw Mt. Etna, I marveled at the beauty of nature's magnificent structure. For some reason, I always felt comfort living at the base of this towering inferno, whether the mountain was covered with snow in the winter months or glowing in the dark of night. I was privileged to be a part of and share this place on our great earth.

"No, the word danger never crossed my mind."

Naval Air Station Sigonella

Naval Air Station Sigonella is located in eastern Sicily, approximately 16 km west of the city of Catania and approximately 24 km due south of Mount Etna. Since its opening, Sigonella has grown to be the premier logistics base in the Mediterranean as it continues to be a vital component in supporting U.S. and NATO operations within the European theater.

Plans to build a naval air facility were drawn up in the early 1950s as a result of an agreement between the U.S. and NATO. Land for Sigonella was made available to the navy on a temporary basis under the terms of an agreement with the Italian government June 25, 1957. The initial building of Sigonella began in September 1957, with the administrative area at NAF I beginning in 1958.

The first Americans arrived at Sigonella in March 1959, but they stayed in Catania except for daily trips to the administrative area because there were no buildings ready for occupancy. During the six months required to make NAF I habitable, the navy occupied the large warehouse complex called Magazine Generale, which is opposite the cemetery on the right side of the street as one enters Catania from the base.

On June 15, 1959, U.S. Naval Air Facility Sigonella was commissioned on top of a field where damaged German fighters and bombers once landed during World War II.

Naval Air Station Sigonella is divided into two bases: NAS I and NAS II. These areas are about a ten-minute drive apart. NAS I was the original base and became the personnel support facility. NAS II is where operational work is conducted.

Frank, Richard, and I lived in Navy Family Housing NAS I. This site included a commissary store, the Navy Exchange Retail Store, grammar school (grades 1 – 6), Naval Hospital and chapel.

NAS II is the Air Field and Operations site and is a joint U.S. and Italian facility with separate supporting areas.

Frank's Job

Frank was a Weapons Officer at NAS II site, which included separate areas for NATO Mine, NATO magazine, and NATO Ordnance areas and U.S. ammunition storage facilities. Provide primary logistical support element for U.S. Sixth Fleet operations throughout Operation Allied Forces. Travels included Augusta Bay Port Facility, Palermo Facility and the island of Crete, Greece.

Martha Lou & Capt. Platt pinning promo bars on Frank - Sigonella, Sicily

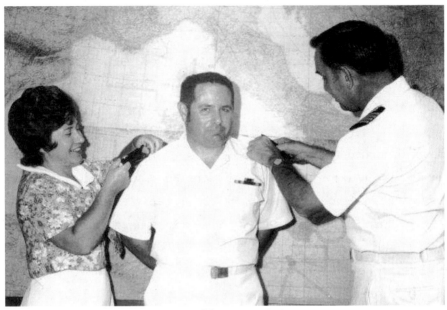

Chapter 24

Sicily

Exhausted from the trip; excitement of arriving soon faded and it took only the ride from the airport to the navy base to show me it was not going to be easy living in Sicily.

Choices: I could cry a lot; missing my family and all the comforts of life that I had been privileged to as an American.

I could be the military wife that I signed on to be. Accept my responsibilities to prepare a loving home for my husband and son and represent my country by doing whatever was required of me to support the mission of my husband.

For me there was no time to ponder these choices. I accepted all the challenges. When my electric appliances didn't work, I beat the meringue with a fork, washed the clothes in the sink, hanging them to dry on a clothes line in the back yard, swept the floors with a broom, dried my hair naturally, and soon came to ignore the electric power outages altogether. I remember going to the commissary daily for food to prepare because our refrigeration was out. I bought mostly fresh vegetables that had been brought to market by Italian farmers. Due to the fertilizers used it was necessary to soak the vegetables in bleach and water and rinse several times.

At first every chore was difficult and annoying, but a strange thing happened to me. I realized I was living the way these Sicilian people had lived for centuries. The more time I spent doing these once annoying tasks, the more free time I seemed to have.

Friends became family; we shared and cared for one another. Our life on the base was filled with events; school, church and social. Off the base we embraced the friendship of several Italian families.

After living there for several months, a Sicilian lady said to me "La Signora, you have caught the Sicilian spirit!"

On holidays and weekends when Frank wasn't working, the three of us climbed into our compact green Fiat and took trips around Sicily. I believe we discovered and explored every historical site on the island.

Richard said he didn't enjoy the rock piles in Sicily. What he remembers today as the most interesting was our trips to Rome, Naples, Venice, Florence, Germany and Switzerland.

The memories we have of being in all these places; seeing Mount Vesuvius in Naples; the works of Michelangelo in Rome and Florence; the canals of Venice; and the Alps of Germany and Austria; all this coupled with the experiences of meeting the people and tasting the food and let us not forget the "shopping."

Wonderful paintings, pottery, embroidery and jewelry; I purchased mostly in Sicily. It was the 1970s, so prices were reasonable then.

My life at Sigonella seemed to take on new meaning as I joined different organizations, involvement in the following: Italian Orphanage; Secretary Youth League; Supervisor of Parent Teachers Organization Thrift Shop; Vacation Bible School teacher; Sunday school teacher; Cub Scout Den Leader, Vice-President Officers' Wives Club of Sigonella, Sicily; Vice President Protestant Women of the Chapel, Sigonella, Sicily and Little Theatre Group.

Three years filled with responsibilities, challenges, triumphs, defeats, joy and heartache; memories that have sustained me for the remainder of my life.

The captain of Sigonella and the American councilor of Sicily told me I should be awarded a medal for all my work. My reply to them, "I am a military wife, reward me, reward them all."

Frank's military orders to Sigonella, Sicily were for a period of two years, but at the end of that time the U.S. Navy extended our stay one year.

Because of the age of my parents, I decided, after the two-year period, I would make the journey from Catania, Sicily to Orlando, Florida.

Two weeks I spent with Mom and Dad. This was the one time in my life that I felt like an only child. Truth, I had nine brothers and sisters, but this visit was all about me and it was special.

They understood that I must leave them again because my place was with my husband and son in Sicily.

The morning I was leaving, Dad said to me, "Is there anything of mine that you would like to have?"

Without hesitation, I replied, "Yes, Dad, I would like to have your pocket watch that you used to put to my ear so I could hear it ticking. That is if you still have it."

After a few minutes, walking out of his bedroom, he handed me the pocket watch.

"I had this watch before you were born. I taught you how to tell time with this watch. Do you remember?"

"I remember, Dad. I remember sitting on your lap, you teaching me the numbers and letting me listen to the ticking."

"Listen to it," he said, "It is still ticking."

"Thanks, Dad." Tears were in his and my eyes.

All that watch ticking had marked the times of all the years passed. I was still his baby daughter.

Traveling occupied a lot of our time during the final twelve months of our stay in Sicily. Being there gave us the opportunity to tour Europe and I took a trip to Tunisia, North Africa.

Our time and travels provided us with great friends and the opportunity to see and do things we never thought possible.

With a Sicilian family we experienced the harvesting of grapes; stomping grapes and wine making. In the countryside, we watched the threshing of wheat, harvesting of olives from the olive trees and picking blood oranges from the orange trees.

Our best friends, Gayle, Delbert, Rodney and Kenny; shared the friendship with the Garilli family.

Whether eating pizza from the Garilli's outdoor pizza brick oven or the American turkey Thanksgiving dinner Gayle and I prepared; the camaraderie transcended differences in language and culture.

These friends whom we found in a foreign land became lifetime companions. Gayle and I played tennis, wearing our white tennis outfits the Sicilian dressmaker made for us. We helped each other when our children were sick and cried with each other when our Sicilian friend died.

Returning to the United States, being stationed in different locations, distance never ended our friendship, not with Gayle and her family or the Garilli family.

❖ **August 1972 Crossing The Alps**- Mountain systems in South Central Europe extending from Southern France through Switzerland, Italy, Southwest Germany, Austria, Slovenia, Croatia, Bosnia and Herzegovina into Yugoslavia; highest peak, Mount Blanc.

❖ **Membership in "The Protestant Women of the Chapel"** – In 1952, the 16th Field hospital organized the first women's chapel group in Europe. That same year the ladies of Nuernburg Post formed a group called "The protestant Women of the Chapel." Since then, this title has been adopted by all of the chapters throughout Europe.

- The theme for the 1956 rally, "Workers Together for Christ," was chosen to become the permanent motto to be incorporated into the official seal. The Darmstadt chapter designed an emblem entwining the letters of PWOC bordered by the motto, "We are Workers Together for Christ." It was adopted by USAREUR as the official emblem for the first time at the fall rally in 1957.

- By 1959, Protestant Women of the Chapel had outgrown its fledgling status; the organizational procedure had been stabilized and the aims clearly stated.

- In 1960, all chapters of the United States Forces, Europe, were united into one organization. The USAREUR Council became the European Council.

- From its inception in 1952, the PWOC chapters now number over 180 at Army, Air Force and Navy installations throughout Europe.

❖ **Father's Pocket Watch** – the make of the watch is Elgin. Age unknown. Martha's first memories of the watch 1945. Today the watch sits in a small glass dome case on a mantle in the home of Martha's son, Richard. Richard is the youngest grandson of Martha's father.

Martha Lou's Dad at home in Florida reading a letter from Sicily.

Letters From Sicily

To: The Family,

 There we stood, Frank, Richard and myself, in the middle of St. Peter's Square, Rome, Italy. It was two days before Christmas 1972 and we had spent fourteen hours in our car traveling from Sicily to Rome. The whisper of rain fell in a light mist upon us and it was chilly.

 The three of us were happy and eager to explore this beautiful city. We marveled at its magnificence. How can I express our feelings when seeing the church of St. Peter's or when gazing at the Sistine Chapel and works of art created by Michelangelo? I felt an appreciation and love shared with those who lived in Rome all those years ago.

 Of course, Richard, upon seeing the Roman Forum and Coliseum, talked about all the Roman battles and Caesar's great days.

 Frank refused to throw a coin in the Fountain of Trevi because of the superstition that those who do so will return to Rome someday. Frank was in Rome eleven years earlier and you guessed it, he did and he did!

*This time Richard and I threw coins in the fountain.
After leaving Rome, we had our
adventurous trip via the old Appian Way
Naples, Italy. We left Naples on
December 31 hoping to be back in Sicily
for the New Year's Eve Midnight Fiesta.*

*There are only two ways to get to
the island of Sicily and those are via
airlines or via boat. Because we were
traveling in Italy with our car, we
naturally were depending on the
Traphgetti (car ferry).*

*We arrived at the place to get
onto the ferry at 2:00 p.m. and the
situation was hopeless. There was a
terrible storm going on in the
Straits of Messina and the ferry was
not running because of the high winds.
So there we sat with about 600 other
cars waiting for the crossing. We
were the only Americans and the only
English speaking people in the group.
The Italians were very hospitable.*

*Twenty minutes till midnight, we
boarded a ferry which was guaranteed
to take us safely across the Straits.
Then it happened. Right there in the
middle of the Messina Straits, 1973 was
born and we celebrated with our Italian
shipmates.*

*Such a beginning to a fantastic
year. We skipped through the month of
January amusing ourselves with
happenings on the base.*

*In February, I became interested in
The PWOC, Protestant Women of the Chapel.
I attended a conference in Naples, Italy
with our local president of the PWOC and
the chaplain from our base. Soon after,
I became vice-president of our group.*

*The winds of March in Sicily were
just a continuation with the rainfall
which had prevailed throughout the winter
months. During this time, I had PWOC,
bowling and in January I became a den
leader in Cub Scouts.*

*For Frank and Richard, January,
February and March were uneventful with
the weather being rainy and them being
outdoors men they just made the best of it.*

*When April and school spring vacation
rolled around we were ready to travel. On
this trip, we enjoyed the company of some
of our friends. We stood in Piazza de
Michelangelo overlooking the beautiful
city of Florence, Italy.*

*Exploring the city, we marveled at
the magnificent works of art, especially
the statue of David, a sculpture by
Michelangelo.*

We didn't leave Florence until I
purchased a charm of the famous Vecchio
Bridge, selecting it from a shop on the
Vecchio Bridge.

One day's travel from Florence took
us to St. Mark's Square, Venice, Italy.
We were fascinated with the canals and
and many bridges connecting the city.

We trod the streets of Venice on
foot, no cars allowed. The atmosphere
has a silence, filled with romance, grace
and charm. Wandering in and out of gay
shops, tasting the excellent food, riding
in the gondolas; all of this while
learning the proud heritage of a world
unto itself.

Leaving Venice, we ventured down the
eastern coast of Italy. We admired the
blue waters of the Adriatic Sea.
Rounding the heel of Italy, we came
upon a delightful small town called
Alverobello. Here the houses have round
roofs and are known as trulli homes.

Crossing monstrous mountains which
presented us with amazing views, we made
our way to the port to get aboard the
Traghagetti. This time we crossed the
Straits of Messina without any problems.

In May I attended a training conference
in Berchtesgaden, Germany.

Little League baseball began in June.
Richard played left field and Frank coached
the team. Their team took first place for
the season.

    My niece, Brenda Kay, came to Sicily
and two days after she arrived our
itinerary was made for a trip in Europe.

    Frank, Richard, Brenda and I
traveled in our green Fiat 124 sedan.
First it was Pompeii, the city that has
been excavated from its burial ground due
to the tremendous eruption of Mt. Vesuvius
in AD 79.

    After a short stay in Caserta, Italy,
we entered Austria. Brenda says that was
her favorite place. The glorious
Bavarian Alps, charming chalets
and delightful waterfalls; easy to under-
stand Brenda's choice.

    North into Germany, we came to
Berchtesgaden. I was happy that I was
returning to share this place with Frank,
Richard and Brenda.

    In the living room of the Eagle's
Nest; glowing fire in the fireplace; we
were told of the owner of this mountain
top tea house. His now infamous name is Hitler.

    Garmisch, Germany was a place we
could have spent several years in;
visiting the Zugspitze Mountain and the

*Neuschwanstein Castle from which Walt
Disney designed his Cinderella Castle.*

*After one night in Vaduz,
Liechtenstein, we were in Switzerland.
White mountaintops, blue skies, rustic
mountain villages, fresh air and a total
healthy feeling; these are my memories of
Switzerland.*

*Coming back into Italy, we bypassed
Milano and Genoa and made our way to Pisa.*

*Yes, the Leaning Tower of Pisa is
"leaning."*

*Richard and I laughed as we remembered
our throwing coins in the Fountain of Trevi
in Rome. Now we were returning to Rome, as
predicted. I have made several visits to
Rome and each time when I leave I have
the feeling I have missed something and I
would like to go back.*

*Naples was our last place to stop in
Italy before returning to Sicily. The
intriguing city of Naples, the real Italy,
we call it. Many, many visits would be
made to Naples during our stay in Sicily.*

*August brought an unfortunate incident.
Frank had an accident in our car. The
car was totaled. Frank was patched up and
back out on the tennis courts before the
insurance bill came in.*

In September, Brenda returned to the
United States; we missed her. School
started for Richard and Little League
football.

November came racing in and before we
knew it, Thanksgiving was here. We shared
our turkey dinner with some Italian friends
and two American families.

Days of December were filled with
holiday events. Frank, Richard and I
attended candlelight service in the base
chapel on Christmas Eve. There with
other military families we thought of
our families back home, of our friends
and our country.

That was our life – 1973 –

Martha

Letter to Mom and Dad

March 25, 1975

Dear Mom and Dad,

I am working in the library tonight from 6 till 9. The librarian is gone on vacation, so I am helping out. Frank and Richard went to the movie. They don't like to stay home when I am not there.

Hope this finds everyone at home well and happy. The three of us are feeling well these days. Richard is happy that he will be out of school one week after Easter. We are looking forward to our trip around Sicily.

As for as we know, we will be transferred to Brunswick, Maine. We will come home first, then drive our car to Maine. I don't know how long we will be able to stay at home. We haven't gotten that far in our planning yet. Frank is still trying to change his orders, but Maine seems to be the place they want to send him. We don't like going back to the cold country, but Frank will be home all the time, so that we are thankful for. Richard is excited about going to Maine, he remembers the snow and ice skating. I am sure we will have a

good time there, but it is so far from
Florida and we wanted to start making
plans for Frank's retirement. We still
hope to be home the first part of July.

I am starting to drop out of
activities on the base so I can get my
house goods in order for shipping. We
have bought a lot of pretty things over
here and I hope everything makes it back
safely – especially us! Ha.

How is Randy's wife getting along?
I think about them a lot and hope some
how everything will work out for the best.

I would like to visit Mildred when we
come home, but if we go to Maine I doubt if
we have enough time to go to see her. I
wish you would tell her that we will be home
in July and see if she could come home at
that time. As soon as I know I will let you
know just what dates we will be home.

We still plan to ship Bingo to Orlando
and he will go in the car wherever we go.

We continue to enjoy life here and I
know we will miss it when we leave. If we
were rich and could come home more often,
I wouldn't mind staying here, but we are not
in the jet set yet!

Well, it is getting close to time to
close the library, so I will sign off and
get going. You two take care and stay out

of trouble. I don't want any bad reports on
you when I get home.

Sending our love –

Always,

Martha, Frank and Richard

P.S.

I overheard Richard and Frank
discussing at the breakfast table this
morning who in the family could make the
best breakfast and they decided that
Colleen could! I tell you they are
anxious to get back to see everyone.

They ask Bingo if he wanted to go
to Florida and he will jump up and bark.
This dog is so spoiled.

Must scoot, Bye

Chapter 25

Returning to the U.S.

What is the greatest challenge a military wife faces? Of course I can not speak for all military wives, but for me the most difficult aspect is dealing with all the farewells. I am not sure that I volunteered for this challenge. The truth is I chose the military life because of my love for Frank, who had dedicated his life to the United States.

Because of Frank's love, comfort and support to his family life, I was able to readily embrace the military way of living. The farewells were easier to handle when Frank and I were together. Not so much when it was him I was saying goodbye to. I do understand that no two spouses are exactly the same, even if they share some common bonds. Therefore there are some wives who love their life and others who hate it.

Remembering the tearful goodbyes when we left Sicily is still emotionally wrenching for me. Farewell to my Sicilian home that for three years encompassed my Sicilian friends, military families and my respect for the Sicilian way of life.

Our time in Sicily had ended. Frank's military orders read: "August 1975 report to Naval Air Station, Brunswick, Maine."

Walking into the Philadelphia airport, Frank, Richard and I were back on American soil.

"Look at all the colors," Richard exclaimed, seeing the neon signs of advertisements and most of the people dressed in bright clothing.

Returning to the United States, we had to adapt to a new reality. All the colors were the least of our worrisome concerns. While Frank had to deal with his command of a new duty station situation, we both were concerned with Richard adjusting to change of school and friends.

Bingo had previously arrived at my sister's house in Orlando. We picked him up; once again, said our goodbyes to Mom and Dad; packed our Chevrolet; bought a new map; here we come: Naval Air Station, Brunswick, Maine.

The best thing about being a military community is you don't have to start from scratch all the time. Most military bases provide facilities such as: hospital, exchange store for clothing, etc. and commissary for food purchases.

Family housing can be difficult to acquire. Not all bases have family housing on the base property and often there is a list of people waiting to move into base housing.

Arriving in Maine, we were wonderfully surprised to have waiting for us a very nice house. Not only base housing, but the kitchen was stocked with groceries. This was military friends taking care of each other. In this case it was Steve, Senior Naval Officer, who became our friend in Sigonella, Sicily.

Thanks to Steve our stay in Maine was off to a good start. August was a great month to arrive in Maine as we had time to prepare before the cold winter months.

We embraced the spectacular weather and scenery of the fall season, September, October and first couple of weeks in November. In November, on Thanksgiving Day, snow began to fall and that was it. We never saw our yard again because we left Maine in March and snow still covered the lawns.

I can't say I enjoyed the cold weather; after all, I am from the South. Living in this cold country was an experience that brought excitement to Richard's life. He readily settled into making new friends and participating in sports activities.

After all these years, he still attributes his ability to read and learn to the elementary school he attended in Brunswick, Maine.

School started, Frank was off to work everyday and many nights of duty station on the base. Finding myself alone, most of the time, I began to search for ways to fight my nagging depression.

Before marriage, I had worked as a bookkeeper and I had a college degree in business. Becoming a military wife and a mother, I had set my career aside. The questions now were should I want to engage in a professional career again, will it be possible?

It was going to be a question of balance. Not just for me but for Frank and Richard. Without their support this was not going to work. After given the green light by both of them, I was on the job search. First things first, shopping for proper attire for working fashion. After all, I needed the fashion in order to create my working-girl attitude.

It worked! After my first interview I got the job! After over a decade of being a stay-at-home mom, I was back in the work force.

Although I readily state that being a mom and a good military wife was first priority for me, I must say that I always needed or intended to be more than someone's "last four numbers." To date, I still readily quote Frank's social security numbers. I have to look up mine.

Surprisingly I found the tasks of the job came easy. Being a military wife, I was familiar with much of the paper work. The job was working in the federal government system located in an office on the naval station.

Not only did I have pride in myself for being back in the work force; I felt an even greater commitment to my country than being a military wife.

Lifetime friendships were made with my office staff and many friends who still live in Maine. Although our time there was short, we have wonderful memories of this special place.

I believe Frank had been misplaced in his position with the navy and was tagged for a new duty station rather quickly.

Springtime in Maine never came for us. I resigned my job, Richard got a school transfer and Frank received his orders.

Take the white curtains down, get ready for the movers, and put suitcases in the car, not forgetting Bingo. Bingo had never been fond of the snow!

The tire chains would stay on the car until we arrived in Pennsylvania. Our destination was as far south as we could go and remain in the United States.

Maine

Maine is the eastern most state of the United States. History reveals the Vikings reached Maine around the year 1000, John Cabot, an English explorer, around 1498. The English established the first permanent settlement in 1607. The territory was part of Massachusetts until 1820, when it became a state. World famous for lobster, Maine is not only a fishing market, but the manufacturer of wood products, especially paper. This is Maine's most important industry. An amazing site to behold is the 17 million acres of forest; land of the most beautiful trees I have ever seen.

Portland, the largest city, and Augusta, the capital, are in the southeast.

Most of the people live in the southeast, within 25 miles of the Atlantic coast. Thousands of people visit the state to ski, fish and hunt.

Brunswick, Maine – settled in 1628 by fishermen, but burned and resettled several times because of wars between the Indians and the English.

Named Brunswick in honor of the House of Brunswick and its scion, King George I; in 1738 incorporated as a town.

Because of the town's location at the head of the massive water falls of the Androscoggin River, there is water power for industry. Major production of lumber and cotton is most noted.

Famous authors who lived in Brunswick: Harriet Beecher Stow, 1850-1852, wrote **Uncle Tom's Cabin**; Nathaniel Hawthorne, class of 1825 of Bowdoin College.

One of the principal employers for Brunswick is the United States Naval Air Station.

Naval Air Station Brunswick – built in 1943, is a military airport for the United States Navy. Located northeast of Brunswick; in use 1943-1946, 1951-present.

Blueberries had been grown on this property that was willed to the needy people of Brunswick.

Today this military base provides a wide range of operations which can be viewed on the web site.

The base is scheduled to close in 2011.

Martha's Employment in Maine – Central Cashier/Payroll Clerk AS-4, U.S. Government, Personnel Support NAS Brunswick, Maine, October 1975-March 1976, Developed User's Guide System for the United States Naval Air Station Personnel Support Department, Brunswick, Maine.

Gerald Ford – President of the United States 1974-1977. Born July 14, 1913 in Omaha, Nebraska; graduate of University of Michigan; he was the Republican leader in the U.S. House of Representatives. In 1973, President Nixon appointed him vice president after then Vice President Spiro Agnew resigned. Then when Nixon resigned the presidency, Ford succeeded him as president in 1974.

He inherited many problems with economics and after the defeat of America's ally, South Vietnam. Also, many Americans were angered when he pardoned President Nixon for any crimes the former president might have committed in office.

He was a Republican and did not get along well with the Democratic controlled Congress.

In 1976, he narrowly lost the presidential election to the Democratic nominee, Jimmy Carter.

Chapter 26

Welcome to Key West

1976, report for duty: Naval Air Station, Key West, Florida.

Going home; it's not just a place, but an emotional feeling. Returning to Florida gave that feeling to Frank, Richard and me. Richard and I stayed in Orlando wit h my sister for a couple of months while Frank attended naval schooling in Virginia.

Richard finished that year of schooling in Orlando and we both enjoyed being with family, especially my mother.

As soon as Frank acquired housing for us, Richard and I joined him in Key West. Once again, we embraced a new way of life. Although I grew up in Florida, I had never been to Key West.

We drove mile after mile of highway and bridges connecting small islands like a chain; the end of the chain; our next duty station.

Together the three of us and Bingo enjoyed the spectacular trip through the Keys. The only circumstance that shadowed this joy of adventure was a dreadful feeling I had when I left the arms of my mother. I could tell she was not well.

Orlando to Key West, 322 miles; a road traveled many times. We were just getting settled in our base housing when the phone call came. Mother was in the hospital.

I try not to remember that painful time. Anyone who has ever had a loved one suffer with that terrible disease, cancer, knows the feeling of helplessness.

The final call came that Mother had passed away. Frank, Richard and I prepared ourselves as best we could. This trip from Key West to Orlando was a very somber time for us.

During my life, I have seen the vision of a beautiful lady, dressed in a long, flowering, pale-blue gown.

Riding in our car, on the way to my mother's funeral, I gazed out the window into the vast, clear-blue sky. I saw my mother all in white, seated in a golden chair.

Around her were several ladies; attending her as they drifted upward in a ring of clouds. The beautiful lady in blue looked at me, giving me such a feeling of comfort.

I said nothing to Frank or Richard. I just said goodbye to Mother.

Continuing our lives without Mother was going to be difficult. I visited my father as often as I could. He was eighty-eight years old and seemed to be doing well.

The warm sun of the South and the easy way of life and friendliness of the people of Key West; all was a blessing in our lives.

Frank concentrated on his military assignment at the Naval Air Station. Richard, chosen to be in one of the first school classes to learn the computer, was intrigued with this learning process. That class was the beginning of a changing educational system for Richard and a changing behavior for all of us.

Playing sports in the Little League program, fishing with his dad and mowing lawns for spending money; Richard was doing well.

After the death of my mother in July, I struggled with my depression. In October I received a call from the Commander of the Special Services of the Naval Air Station, Key West. His job offer came at a perfect time for me. I had enjoyed my work in Maine and now I could continue in Key West.

Memories of the time in Key West are filled with the warmth of not only the sunshine, but of dear friends, fun sports and easy living.

There is a saying, "All good things come to an end."

Frank was facing a decision that would change our lives. There is another saying that fits this situation: "Hold on, you are in for a bumpy ride."

Martha Lou & Frank attend social event at the
U.S. Naval Air Station, Key West, Florida

Martha Lou & Lt. Frank Perritti, Jr.
Retirement Ceremony U.S. Navy Station, Orlando, Florida

Chapter 27

Retirement

During one's lifetime, there are crossroads. In 1977, the choice of which road to take was Frank's decision. He had joined the United States Navy in 1956 and now, twenty-one years later, he could retire.

Knowing that his next set of orders, after his Naval Air Station, Key West, Florida, would be sea duty; his main consideration was being separated from his son. Richard was now fourteen years old and Frank's number-one priority was to be with him during his teenage years.

Frank, Richard and I spent hours discussing what our life would be like after the military years.

Richard's comments included: "No more guards at the gate. No more saying goodbye to Dad at the pier as the ship sails to sea. No more constant sound of planes soaring over the house."

We agreed that having a permanent home where Richard could attend the same high school until graduation and maintain high school friendships would be so important to giving him a good education.

Worrisome factors included being separated from the military community that anchored our family, giving instant camaraderie. Leaving our comfort zone would require courage from all three of us.

Frank was concerned with his being able to find a job. He wasn't sure how much he would need to make in order to sustain his family. He was sure his retirement pay was not going to be enough.

Once we left Key West, I would be giving up my job with the government and had no idea what I could find elsewhere.

For sure, there was no one knocking on our door to tell us about resources that were available or give us a plan.

Always before, the military orders were our road map; this time we must write our own set of orders. To take advantage of military retirement benefits, we needed to live near a military base to utilize the medical and commissary facilities.

With determination not to be afraid and to be flexible, the three of us faced this part of life called retirement.

The rules of the military no longer apply. The trick is to enjoy the passing of the guard. From now on, we will be the script writer of the day.

Exploring our options, decisions were made and once our course was set, the three of us and Bingo were on the road again. Bumpy ride or not, it was our future.

Key West

Key West is the county seat of Monroe County, Florida, United States. Located 129 miles southwest of Miami, Florida and 106 miles north-northeast of Havana, Cuba. The city Key West encompasses, Key West, the namesake island.

Key West is known as the southern most city in the continental United States. Inhabited by the Calusa people in pre-Columbian times; the first European known to visit was Juan Ponce de Leon in 1521. As Florida became a Spanish colony, the Spanish called the island of Key West, Cayo Hueso.

In 1763, the British took control of Florida, but 20 years later, Florida returned to Spanish control. After the United States declared its independence, ownership of Key West was transferred several different times. Because of the island's strategic location, it was considered the "Gibraltar of the West." This area provided ships wide deep shipping lanes, through the Straits of Florida, between the Atlantic Ocean and the Gulf of Mexico.

It is no wonder that salvage of wrecked ships made Key West the largest and richest city in Florida and the wealthiest town per capita in the United States. After the American Civil War, the salvage industries declined. During the war, Florida seceded from the Union, but Key West remained in Union hands because of the naval base. Several forts were constructed from 1845 to 1866. One of the most noted, Fort Jefferson, served after the Civil War as the prison for Dr. Samuel A. Mudd, convicted of conspiracy for setting the broken leg of John Wilkes Booth, the assassin of President Abraham Lincoln.

Key West remained relatively isolated until 1912 when it was connected to the Florida mainland via the Overseas Railway extension of Henry M. Flagler's Florida East Coast Railway. After most of the railroad was destroyed by a hurricane in 1935, the U.S. government rebuilt the rail route as an automobile highway. This extension of United States Highway 1, through the Keys is called the Overseas Highway. It is the only road available to travel in and out of the Keys.

Time Line of History

♦ **1926** – Pan American Airlines was founded in Key West, originally to fly visitors to Havana, Cuba.

♦ **1959** – Cuban revolution; the Cuban Missile Crisis; U.S. cut travel and aid to Cuba.

♦ **1982** – Mariel Boatlift refugees came to Key West from Cuba.

♦ **2003** – Refugees continue to come – one hijacked Cuban Airlines plane flew into the city's airport.

♦ **Today** – Watching the sunset at Mallory Square; touring the homes of famous writers; Ernest Hemingway and Tennessee Williams; exploring all the historical sites; shopping; come on a cruise ship or drive the Overseas Highway; experience the enchantment of Key West.

Naval Air Station Key West, 1823 – Established for the purpose of stopping piracy in the area. Operations expanded during the Mexican-American War and the Spanish-American War in 1898. World War I (1914-1918) brought another expansion to block German ships and train student aviators.

After World War I, the base was decommissioned and remained inactive until 1939. America's entry into World War II called for a state of emergency, reopening the Naval Base Key West to support war efforts. With our fighting the war by air and sea; the base became a strategic location.

In March 1945, after the war was won, the base was designated as U.S. Naval Air Station, Key West. Permanently etched in military history, the base continues to be used for training and a primary staging base for needed operations.

Martha's Employment – Administrative/Accounting Section Special Service Branch AS-5, Naval Air Station, Key West, Florida (October 1976-April 1977)

Computer Introduced to Richard and the Education System – In 1946, the first computer was developed by engineer Presper Eckert and physicist John Mauchly. 1970s, the computer changed the way people communicated and played and also how they worked and learned.

Martha's Mother – (1902 – 1976) – Began her life in the Warrior Mountains of North Alabama. Married at the age of 18, gave birth to 10 children. Died of cancer; buried in Caddo Cemetery, Alabama. The story of her ancestors is told in Martha Lou Perritti's book *Standing Against the Wind.*

Frank's Retirement Orders:

♦ August 1, 1977

♦ Honorable Service United States Navy

♦ August 1956 – August 1977

♦ **1956** – Enlisted Tampa, Florida

♦ **(1956 – 1959)** San Diego, California

- Norman, Oklahoma
- Jacksonville, Florida
- Chincoteague, Virginia

♦ **(1960 – 1962)** Heavy Attack

- Squadron One
- Naval Air Station
  - Sanford, Florida

♦ **(1960 – 1962)** Included Sea Duty on

- USS Independence

♦ **(1962 – 1965)** Naval Air Station

- Sanford, Florida
  - Weapons Department

♦ **(1965 – 1967)** Naval Air Station

- Heavy Attack Squadron Twelve
- Weapons
- Branch LCPO
- Naval Air Station
  - Pensacola, Florida
- Training (WOINDOC)
- NATTC
  - Jacksonville, Florida
  - Training (ORD.ADMIN)

- **(1967 – 1970)** Naval Station
  - Roosevelt Roads, Puerto Rico
    - Weapons Department
- **(1970 – 1972)** USS WASP
  - Ordnance Handling
  - Air Gunner
- **(1972 – 1975)** USNAF Sigonella
  - Sicily
  - NATO Magazines
- **(1975 – 1976)** Naval Air Station
  - Brunswick, Maine
  - GSE
- **(1976 – 1977)** Naval Air Station
  - Key West, Florida
  - Weapons Officer
- **Promotions:** 1965 – Chief Petty Officer
  - 1967 – Commissioned WO-1
  - 1970 – Lt. JG
  - 1972 – Lt.
    - Orlando, Florida
    - Retirement

PART
III

Chapter 28

Transition

Setting goals for our lives had been the keystone of our marriage. Now that Frank's commitment of service in the military had ended, he focused his unique ability of planning on our future. As always, he continued to provide Richard and me the highest level of support possible. Our new home, north of Orlando, was like a dream come true.

The final destination for our household goods was determined: a retirement ceremony in Key West; then one last retirement event was held at the Officer's Club, United States Naval Station, Orlando, Florida.

Looking at my husband in his distinctive naval officer's uniform, I was so very proud of his accomplishments. Upon Frank's retirement from his military duties, I could only stand aside and hope that my role as his military wife would be respected.

Throughout the years and at every duty station, I did my best to make a difference by getting involved; taking on leadership responsibilities of the military communities. Always reaching out to help others, I never lost sight of enjoying every step of the way.

At the end of this journey, I carry the deepest appreciation for the opportunities provided to me as a military wife. Because of Frank's job and mission, I explored parts of the world that otherwise I would have never experienced.

Traveling and meeting different people gave me the chance to touch people lives as they did mine. I will forever cherish our military friendships and memories of times shared will not fade.

"The End," not so! Frank's military retirement opened our recognition of life outside the military and made us look at the scenario of civilian life. The military life had been our anchor. Now we must find a new perspective for our future and a passion to sustain it.

The excitement of moving into our first "real" home was shared with family and friends. Our first priority was to help Richard adjust to changing schools and friends. This was made easier because of our sense of security in knowing Daddy wasn't going anywhere and there would be no more orders to move.

It was awesome to watch as Frank transformed into a civilian. Without hesitation, he started his own business in landscaping. Gone were the days of taking orders, wearing the same uniform everyday and constant responsibility of duty. Now he was his own boss and he rapidly succeeded, enjoying his newfound freedom.

It was a beautiful neighborhood. Frank, Richard and Bingo seemed happy and all was well. I am not sure if I should reveal this, but I think other military wives will understand. Loneliness is the word that comes to mind when I think back on the days following Frank's retirement and our settling down in a permanent community. Our non-military neighbors seemed undisciplined and lacking purpose. The military community was always so focused on fighting for freedom, keeping America safe. My newfound friends seemed not to share these concerns. In order not to be isolated, I knew I was going to have to be flexible in following this new path.

I no longer had what I referred to as my military duties, so what did I still have? My responsibilities as a wife and mother and oh yes, there was my career. If Frank could change job directions, so could I.

In 1977, I became the credit manager/office manager for Jacobson's, an exclusive department store located near our home in Longwood, Florida.

Martha Lou & her father Ruben Killgore at her
grandfather's grave in Tallapossa, Georgia

Chapter 29
The Good Life

I was sure I was living in "the best of times." Frank was doing
well with his new business; Richard had many good friends and seemed
happy in school; at work I had good friends and I loved my job. All this
with living in a beautiful new home, lovely neighborhood; even Bingo
enjoyed his half-acre yard.

Dad was now ninety years old. Trying to spend as much time with him as I could, we went on several trips. At the time, I had no clue as to how important these trips with my dad would become to me.

When I was spending time in Tallapoosa, Georgia, Dad told me about his younger years there. Standing beside his papa's grave, he showed me the grave headstone that he and his brother had carved using a nail. The stone was found in the woods nearby. When he replaced that stone with a modern marble headstone, he gave me the nail-carved one. Now, thirty one years later, this stone rests in my flower garden at my front door. The nail etching still visible: D 1913 F M Kilgore.

So much time shared with my dad, telling me stories of his life; reciting poetry he had memorized in school; all now cherished memories. Although I would later find out that some of the things he told me about his life were not the truth, I don't fault him for trying to do what he thought was right.

From the first time Dad saw my son, Richard, he told me many times what a special child he was.

"Daughter," he said, "you take care of that boy. He's going to be somebody."

As the years passed, Dad watched Richard grow. So impressive was Dad when he gave a speech to Richard's history class in high school. He spoke for over an hour about his experiences during World War I. The students were spell-bound by this ninety-five-year-old man and Richard was extremely proud. This was his grandfather!

Richard's high school graduation was celebrated with his grandfather attending. Choosing to finish a two-year degree at Seminole Junior College, then entering the United States Air Force; Richard's independence had been declared.

Grandfather was not the only one proud of him. Frank and I were so pleased with Richard's accomplishments and now we must have faith that his future would have many successes.

I know the old saying "you have to let your children go," but Frank and I were asking, "Why does he have to go so far away?"

Richard's first duty station in the Air Force was in Athens, Greece (1985-1987). We lived in constant fear because of this turbulent time of terrorist attacks.

Richard Perritti, Reuben Killgore & Martha Lou Perritti
"Dad's Orange Grove" – Orlando, Florida

Chapter 30

Illness Returns

I am not sure when it happened, but I thought my life was just about perfect. Spending my days working at Jacobson's with people I enjoyed; coming home to a loving husband; surrounded with my son's laughter and Bingo's constant greeting; I not only don't know when it happened; I don't know why it happened.

The illness I had suffered from before, anxiety/depression, returned with a vengeance. One day I was at work; Richard in high school; Frank managing his lawn business, the next day I could no longer function well enough to do my job or participate in my home life.

Doctors asked me to explain how I was feeling. Then when I did, they just gave me a blank stare. No one seemed to understand as I kept sliding into a dark place.

When I wasn't going from doctor to doctor, I stayed in bed most of the time. Finally I remembered a medicine that my doctor in Rhode Island had given me the first time I suffered from this illness. My current doctor did not hesitate to give me a prescription and within days I was on my way to recovery. Now I take this medicine every day of my life.

By the time Richard graduated from high school, I was back to being myself again. I did give up my job with Jacobson's, but had no trouble in finding activities in which to get involved.

They say hard times in your life make you a stronger person. After going through that period of illness, I am not sure about being stronger, but now I have faith that no matter how bad situations are, things can turn around and get better.

Frank and I missed our son being at home with us and it was so difficult realizing he was in a danger zone living in Greece; being in the Air Force.

The 1980s had presented me with challenges; overcoming a lingering illness, Richard graduating from high school and junior college and joining the Air Force, leaving home.

The one thing in my life that never changed was the devotion of my husband.

Whether it was the military life, sickness, good times or bad times or missing Richard; we faced everything together.

History of the Times

From 1977 to 1981

President of the United States – James Earl (Jimmy) Carter, Jr., a Democrat, governor of Georgia (1971-1975), elected 39th president of the United States.

His honest, easygoing manner made him popular in the White House. He used his communication skills in foreign affairs; bringing Prime Minister Begin of Israel and President Sadat of Egypt together to sign a historic peace treaty; signing a treaty known as SALT 2, limiting nuclear weapons with the Soviet Union.

Iran took 63 Americans hostage, Carter's military mission to rescue them failed. After that his popularity declined. He lost the next election although the hostages were released on Carter's last day of office.

From 1981 to 1989

United States President Ronald Wilson Reagan, Republican, one of the most popular presidents in U.S. history. He increased defense spending, maintained a strong anti-Soviet, anti-Communist stand; ordered U.S. troops to invade the Caribbean nation of Grenada; supported guerilla forces in Nicaragua; supplied weapons to rebel forces in Afghanistan; ordered U.S. planes to bomb Libya.

Reagan's presidency was marked by increasing budget deficits and trade deficits. He was in office for eight years.

The Healing Wall – November 13, 1982

The Healing Wall is a V-shaped wall of black marble engraved with the names of the more than 58,000 Americans who were killed in Vietnam or died later from their wounds; dedicated the Vietnam Veterans Memorial, Washington D.C.; came to be known as "The Wall."

This memorial symbolizes a new era of national reconciliation of everyone honoring the dead without judging the Vietnam War itself. "The Wall" is among the most visited sites in Washington, D.C. by people from all over the world.

Top Hit: Thriller – 1984, Michael Jackson

Events that shape the history of America are not always those of government, manufacturers or organizations but by individuals who propel themselves into greatness.

Age 5, Michael Jackson began singing with his family. In 1979 he began doing solo albums and his popularity began to grow. His singing and dancing created an unbelievable sensation.

His album, Thriller, came out in 1982 and by 1984 it was the best-selling album in history. This galvanizing performer passed away in 2009.

Space Tragedy – 1986

My son, Richard was in the United States Air Force, serving in Athens, Greece. He had asked his dad and me to sell his car because he would be in Greece for two years and did not need his car.

The morning of January 28, 1986 preparations had been made to meet the person at our local bank to sell the car for Richard. Frank drove Richard's car and I followed in our car.

We had watched on TV, the progress of the Challenger shuttle launch into space from Cape Canaveral and planned to be outside when it lifted off because we could see it in the sky due to the fact we lived only fifty miles away.

There was a delay in lift-off. When I got in my car, I turned the radio on as I was driving. I heard the NASA spokesperson say, "We have lift-off. Go with throttle up."

I looked into the sky out the windshield of my car and I saw the shuttle explode, spraying smoke and debris to earth. "Surely they got out," I repeated to myself as I heard no confirmation on the radio. Traffic was pulling over alongside the roads. I continued to the parking lot of the bank where Frank was waiting. He took me in his arms saying, "They are all lost. Did you see it?"

I have never experienced anything like it; people were hugging each other, crying, praying, strangers coming together in their grief.

President Reagan spoke to the nation about Challenger's heroes: "We will never forget them, nor the last time we saw them, this morning, as they ... waved good-bye and slipped the surly bonds of earth 'to touch the face of God.'

Space Program

The Soviet Union sent the first Sputnik into orbit around the earth in 1957. On May 5, 1961 the first U.S. astronaut was launched into space. Alan B. Shepard, Jr. boarded the Freedom 7 space capsule and made his historical 15-minute suborbital flight.

1962, John H. Glenn was the first American to orbit the earth. 1969, Neil A. Armstrong and Edwin E. Aldrin, Jr. landed on the moon. Space travel was done in the Apollo capsules until 1981 when the U.S. introduced the first reusable space vehicle. The space shuttle in space travel became a regular occurrence.

The complacency vanished when, 73 seconds after Challenger lifted off in 1986, burning gases escaped from a defective seal in one of the booster rockets igniting an explosion that destroyed the shuttle, killing all aboard.

Space travel continues with the promise to land an astronaut on Mars before 2019.

Cold War

This term describes the tension between democratic and communist countries that began after World War II. Both sides built up large military arsenals and the world was on the brink of nuclear destruction.

The Cuban Missile Crises of 1962, the Korean War and the Vietnam War – all conflicts over communist rule.

On March 1983 when the president of the United States Ronald Reagan, called the Soviet Union the "evil empire," the cold war was in a frigid phase. Ronald Reagan was the most anti-Soviet American president.

In 1985, the Soviets gained a new, young leader, Mikhail Gorbachev, and that changed everything.

These two leaders came together on December 8, 1987 and signed a treaty that laid the ground work for ending the cold war. The INF Treaty – the Intermediate-Range Nuclear Forces Treaty eliminated an entire class of atomic weapons.

The Berlin Wall

By 1989 reforms initiated by Mikhail Gorbachev opened the borders to communist countries and their people were free to travel.

Perhaps the most imposing symbol of the Cold War was the Berlin Wall. Built in 1961 to halt the flight of East Germans to the west, the 28-mile long barrier performed its function with brutal efficiency.

The wall stood for almost three decades as hundreds of people died trying to cross it to freedom. On November 9, 1989, the leader of East Berlin's Communist Party announced that at midnight East Germans would be free to leave the country. The passage way through the wall was opened as thousands shouted "Tor auf!" ("Open the gate!"), then streamed into West Germany.

In a speech given by the United States President Ronald Reagan, he asked Gorbachev to "tear down that wall." The wall was torn down mostly by Berliners, then construction crews. People from all over the world have pieces of the wall which serve as a reminder of the hated barrier.

My nephew, Keith, gave me a piece of the wall and I have it in my office. I pick it up now and again, somehow feeling the power of freedom.

Chapter 31

Threats of Terrorism

Richard's first duty station as a United States Air Force military man was Athens, Greece.

When after two years, his transfer to the U.S. was turned down; Frank and I were prepared to travel to Greece.

Because of terrorist attacks in that part of the world, we were warned of the danger in our travel plans. "Mom, don't come to Greece," Richard's words as he explained over the phone, he would be coming home on leave. Leave meant he would be returning to Greece, but we were not going to think about that.

Standing in the Orlando airport, watching arrivals from New York, we searched for Richard.

"Mom, it's me," I heard a so familiar voice. My son, the United States Air Force military man, had hair down to his collar, a Greek leather jacket, jeans and boots.

Once we got home, he explained his attire was all by design so that he could not be recognized as an American. Being Italian made for the perfect disguise, black hair, and olive skin tone; just don't talk to anyone!

Flying aboard a Greek airline to New York, upon his arrival he got in line for customs inspections. The officer at the gate questioned, "Do you have anything to declare?"

Before Richard's answer, the officer asked, "Are there any Americans on this flight?"

Richard removed his left shoe, lifted the sole flap and pulled out his United States military identification card.

The gate keeper reached out to shake Richard's hand, "Welcome home, son!"

Sitting alone at my kitchen table, listening to my son and my husband talking and laughing. I began to cry. I was relieved that my son was home and concerned that in our world United States military men had to hide their identity because of the threat of terrorism.

Reading the newspaper, I became more despondent over terrorist attacks by radicals and on top of this, reports of greedy Americans causing scandals on Wall Street in New York City.

It was just the beginning. Radical terrorism would come ashore; our financial markets would come to the brink of collapsing.

Do you understand the tears, as I hugged my only son goodbye at the airport; sending him back into harm's way?

He was a military man, just like his father. The saying still rang true, "Martha, you are marrying a United States military man. The duties of the military will come first – you will be second."

Watching Frank's face now, over twenty years later saying good-bye to our son, I realized the statement had changed, slightly. I was now priority number three.

That was okay. With all the fear, pride loomed; trust and faith prevailed. Our son survived to come home again. Our country is still struggling.

Picture on following page:

Richard Victor Perritti – U.S. Air Force 1985

Richard Perrittti escorts his grandfather Reuben Killgore at
Reuben's 100th birthday celebration.

Chapter 32
Loneliness and Death

Dealing with the loneliness of having our only child not only gone from home, but so far away in another country; we were afraid of so many things.

As together we tried to figure out our future; a knock on our front door changed everything.

Gordon walked into our lives. Frank had worked for Gordon for several years doing lawn maintenance and landscaping. Gordon had built a multimillion-dollar house in Windermere, just south of Orlando. His proposal to us was: he would build a house of our choice across the street from his in Windermere; we would live there rent free and he would give Frank a generous salary to maintain his property. Although we loved our home, we had moved into after retirement from the military and shared such a good life with our son; the thing we needed most at this time, was change. If this meant moving, we certainly knew how to do that. Just like all the times before we would take our memories with us.

By April 11, 1988, our life was blessed with our son stationed in the state of Oklahoma and on this date, we celebrated my father's 100th birthday.

The Officer's Club at the United States Naval Base in Orlando, Florida hosted a grand celebration to honor my dad.

Richard, wearing his United States Air Force uniform, proudly escorted Dad through the celebration procedures.

It was an amazing experience to be with Dad at this age in his life. To this day, I cherish all the times we shared.

April 11, 1989, Dad's 101st birthday was celebrated with just his immediate family. He was beginning to die of old age.

It was traumatic to let go of the person who had the greatest impact on my life. Fifty years, there had always been Dad, somewhere in my life.

Standing beside his grave in Caddo Cemetery, so many different emotions, one that lingered; I was saying good-bye to a stranger. How could that be?

Chapter 33

War – Cory's Letter – Facts

Losing my mother in 1976 was terrible, but I had Dad for thirteen years to hold on to. Once Dad was gone, that was the end of the family unity. There would be no more Christmas trees with the small brown sacks underneath.

I tried for several years to keep this tradition going but ultimately it fell apart.

As always, I turned to my husband for happier times. Our life living across the street from Gordon in Windermere was the perfect choice for us. We had a beautiful home, Frank enjoyed his work and we were able to travel to Oklahoma to visit Richard.

Still in the Air Force, Richard enrolled in the University of Central Oklahoma. Previously he had finished two years of junior college and taken classes offered by the University of Maryland while stationed in Greece.

In 1989, we attended his graduation from the University of Central Oklahoma. Richard made his decision to get out of the Air Force and return to Florida for employment.

For a get-away place, Frank and I bought a condo on Pine Island, near Fort Myers, Florida. We used it for vacation, but that was about to change.

Richard became the Records Manager for Lee County, Fort Myers, Florida. He moved into our condo. When we went down for our vacation days, he was there and it was wonderful.

Then the phone call came. The United States Government gave notice to Richard to report for active duty in the Air Force. His commitment to serve had continued; his uniform ready, he waited for orders.

United States troops were deployed to the Mideast nation of Kuwait for the purpose of freeing Kuwait from occupation by its neighbor Iraq.

"A line drawn in the sand," President Bush called the January 15, 1991 date given to Iraq to withdraw from Kuwait. Iraq stepped across that line, brought on the fighting, by continuing to occupy Kuwait.

January 16, 1991, the Persian Gulf War began. Before it was over the Allied military death toll was 224. By February 27, only 100 hours after the beginning of the ground war, Kuwait was liberated.

Because of the ending of the war in a short period of time, Richard was not deployed to the Mideast.

Realizing how fortunate we were that our son was not in harm's way, I wrote letters to others who were. I know how important mail from home was when I lived overseas. Without a doubt men and women in combat zones appreciate their mail.

03Feb91

Martha and Frank,
Thanks so much
for taking the time to let
me know I'm in your
thoughts and prayers.
American Red Cross
You both know how mail
brightens your day!
Things here are hectic and tense, but for the most part we have

avoided most of the "fireworks." My battalion is extremely
Busy supporting various Marine units on the Kuwait/Saudi
border, so we have had pretty good seats for the show. But
being busy leaves little time for thinking about where we're at and
what we're up against, that probably keeps us sane. Spirits are
good and the support from the States keeps it going.

Living conditions are pretty primitive by
any standards, but we make ourselves as comfortable
as we can. You'd be amazed at what makes us happy these days!

All in all, I'm doing well and there's at
least a light in the tunnel – I'll get to go home
to Shelia- around a July time frame. (That's what keeps me
going!)

Should Richard be sent over, please let me
know and I'll try to get in touch with him, if I
can. Extended family is fantastic support – and
you and yours certainly are family. Two generations worth!

All this will be over sooner than we think,
so I'll keep hanging in here – Friends like both
of you make it easy!

Take Care,

Cory

Credit Manage/Office Manager – Jacobson's Department Store, Longwood, Florida (1977-1983). This was a stressful job at times, but I have good memories of friendships with the employees and customers.

Terrorism – The use of violence to achieve some goal.

When my son was deployed to Greece following his enlistment into the United States Air force, the fear of terrorism consumed me. I knew that acts of terrorism were happening all over the world.

Terrorist groups were hijacking airplanes, assassinating people, kidnapping hostages, and planting bombs.

In 1979, the U.S. Embassy was seized in Iran and dozens of Americans were taken hostage. The final 52 were not freed until 1981.

In 1983, terrorists bombed the headquarters of an international peacekeeping force in Lebanon. Nearly 200 American and French soldiers were killed; many asleep in their barracks.

My son survived the constant threat of terrorism during his deployment with the U.S. Air Force; some Americans were not so lucky.

George Bush – President of the United States (1989-1993)

Served as vice president under Ronald Reagan (1981-1989). Put together a 28-nation military coalition to make Iraq leader, Saddam Hussein, withdraw from Kuwait. This war, known as Desert Storm, was successful.

In 1990, he backed a bill in Congress to reduce the deficit by raising taxes. This was after, when running for president, he promised "no new taxes."

This and a declining national economy were factors in his loss of the presidential election in 1992.

The Persian Gulf War (1991) – also known as Desert Storm.

On August 2, 1990, the forces of Iraqi dictator Saddam Hussein invaded Kuwait, a tiny country located north of the strategic oil fields of Saudi Arabia. This move put Iraq in a position to choke off much of the world's energy supply.

When sanctions on Iraq didn't convince them to leave Kuwait, the American-led coalition gave Saddam Hussein an ultimatum: Either quit Kuwait by January 16, 1991 or face eviction by force.

When the deadline passed without response, the attack got underway. On January 17, hundreds of aircraft pressed the attack. Cruise missiles and radar-evading Stealth fighter planes destroyed targets in the city and elsewhere. They pounded Iraqi positions in advance of what Saddam promised would be the "mother of all battles."

Failing to live up to his rhetoric, the Iraqi forces were defeated after a 100-hour ground attack. Kuwait was liberated.

Little Brown Sacks – 1989, the end of a family tradition.

Before I was born in 1939, my mother and father started this family tradition that lasted through fifty years of my life.

The little brown sacks, filled with fruit and candy, were placed underneath our Christmas tree on Christmas Eve. Each sack had the name of a child written on the fold down top. No matter how old or young, each member of the family received a "little brown sack."

The story goes "the stockings were hung by the chimney with care"; in our case, because my parents could not afford to buy the stockings, they used little brown sacks.

When I got older, helping my dad fill the sacks; this is my happiest memories of Christmas.

After my dad's death, I tried to continue the tradition, but I came to realize that this tradition didn't mean as much to my siblings as it did to me.

Christmas morning, Mom, Dad, little brown sacks under the tree, memories of my life.

Chapter 34

Change and Dreams

My life as a military wife had been filled with challenges and changes. Some were dramatic; some not so much, all weaving a web through the years of my life.

When Frank and I moved across the street from Gordon, the comment was made, "Gordon and Frank will live here, growing old together." This was not my comment, because I knew life with Frank and me was all about change and that always meant moving.

1990 brought about several health problems for Frank. Richard had the son to father talk, "Dad, it's time you give up your job, move into your condo on Pine Island, play tennis and go fishing."

Without any argument we began to pack. The main reason for our move to Pine Island was for Frank's health, but I was absolutely thrilled to embrace the "island life."

Richard moved out of the condo and into Ft. Myers; Frank and I moved into the condo and bought a boat!

Living the blissful life, vacation style, for several months, something seemed to be missing. Frank packed his lawn equipment on his small gray trailer and started taking care of lawns in several areas of the island. Now he still had his work with the bonus of playing tennis and fishing.

What about me? The distance in driving into Ft. Myers to continue my job with Jacobson's was not manageable; burnt out with social life after over twenty years as a military wife; didn't like fish (not eating them or catching them); the boat was good for a leisure ride once in a while.

The waves splashed against the rock I was sitting on; flight of the osprey as she called her young; sounds and sights of Charlotte Harbor on the shores of Pine Island, I questioned, what is next for me?

If you are lucky to reach a point in your life when you have the choice to follow a dream that has been hidden within you; take a chance.

Trying to please my parents, living with them for twenty three years; being the best military wife I knew to be; a devoted mother of my son; always giving my time to others; could it be possible for me to make that choice, to take that chance; to follow my dream?

From as far back as I can remember I loved books. There were few books in our house. Before I was old enough to go to school, I would gather my brother's and sister's school books, stack them around me and pretend I was reading them. I didn't know what a library was until after I had been in grammar school for several years.

Reading was like a miracle for me. Quickly I realized that most everything I needed to know I could read in a book. Once I could go to the library, I would walk the aisles touching all the books; I would often take books from the shelves and stack them around me on a table.

In those early years, I developed a dream. A deep, lonely dream, that never went away. My vision of a book on one of those shelves in the library written by me; me, an author; it was only a dream.

Walking along the shore of Charlotte Harbor; wandering around the condo complex past the tennis courts and swimming pool; I am fifty years old. Is there a chance I can make my dream come true? Shall I take that chance?

Talking to myself, I laid out the facts. Son's living his independent life; husband retired naval officer out fishing and playing tennis; small condo, doesn't require much housekeeping; what was my role now?

One thing for sure, age does matter. If I am ever going to write a book, it's time to get started.

There, I said it aloud, "I am going to write a book!"

Next question, "How do I do that?"

Richard Victor Perritti – Pine Island, Florida

Chapter 35

"Cooking Our Way"

The perception others have of you is the role you play in life. Mine was "military wife." That would have been the beginning and the end had I not lived past age fifty.

Taking a long look at myself in the mirror, I struggled with thoughts of what to do. I had been given a chance to make a choice; to play a different role in life. As with everything I had worked on and accomplished in my lifetime, I now made this decision.

After a few minutes, calmness came; my mind caught up with my heart. My harbored dream of becoming an author would come true.

I had no idea of how to start to make this happen. Seeking advice, I called Sheila. Sheila is like a daughter to me. Her mother, Kay, is my dear friend from the years we spent in Puerto Rico as military wives. Sheila was now an editor, very accomplished in her field of work.

Once I expressed to Sheila my desire to write, she became my motivator. I confessed to her that I had no formal training in journalism. The closest thing to writing a book I had done was putting together a cookbook for the Naval Officers' Wives Club.

She pounced on that. "Go with that," she says, "you will get your feet wet by using your organizational skills and creativity."

Relentlessly I worked on my cookbook until it was complete, published and I held "***Cooking Our Way***" in my hands.

What happened next was totally unexpected. People, strangers, wanted to buy my cookbook. Store owners wanted to sell it in their stores.

In 1993, I was in the marketing business, selling a cookbook I created. Sixty-two different shops sold my books. I was doing book signings and cooking classes.

I had succeeded in changing my role in life. I am not sure what my husband's thoughts were when I began working on my cookbook. I do know that once I proved my commitment to writing and produced a tangible object that was making money; Frank became very supportive. He and my son, Richard, had accepted this person I had become. Holding on to the love and support of my husband and my son I had entered into a new commitment in my life. Most of my time was now spent in marketing my cookbook.

Public attention was gratifying and I did feel the satisfaction of accomplishment, having published **"Cooking Our Way."**

How wise is Sheila? Taking her advice to create my cookbook I had deepened my desire to write a book of another genre. I had the confidence that I could do this, or at least I could try, and mostly the discipline of my time was now in good order.

Okay, I was there, ready to write my story. Questions, what do I write about? Without hesitation I turned to Sheila.

"On choosing a subject to write about and as a beginning author; write about something you know. For you, Martha, I suggest you write about your dad. He lived to be 101 years old and his life through 100 years of history would be interesting to readers all over the world."

Hanging up the phone, I repeated what I said to Sheila, "I'll think about it."

After Dad died (1989) I had dismissed my wondering about his life – that is the part I didn't know.

Burying him, I remember feeling as if I were saying goodbye to a stranger. How could I possibly write his life's story when I didn't know it?

Several weeks passed as I gathered all the items I had that belonged to Dad; his hat, pocket watch, letters, photos, etc.

Recalling stories he had told me, I jotted them down on notebook paper. Born in 1888; married my mother, 1920; thirty two years of his life were missing from my knowledge except for the few stories he had told me.

"Hi, Sis" was the way my conversation began, "Can you tell me anything about Dad's life before he met and married Mother?"

"Why?" she replied.

"Because I want to write a book about Dad, but nothing is coming together because there is so much of his life that I don't know."

"Martha Lou," she said, "Another sister and I have been doing a lot of research on Dad's life and if it is okay with her, you are welcome to come along. Together we will find out the secrets of our dad's life."

And so our journey began.

Crossing in the Rain

by

Martha Lou Perritti

Chapter 36

"Crossing In The Rain"

Joining forces, the three of us, sometimes with another sister, took trips, spent hours pouring over census records, searching library shelves, demanding records from courthouses and funeral homes. We wrote numerous letters to government agencies. We walked graveyards and sought out the living to speak the truth.

Rather quickly our search began to reveal the mysterious, hidden life of our dad. Many visits to Tallapoosa, Georgia helped establish the story of the family into which Dad had been born. Time spent in Tallapoosa, Georgia; Sanford, Florida; Decatur, Alabama; Jeffersonville, Indiana; Louisville, Kentucky; Jacksonville, Florida; Birmingham, Alabama; and Orlando, Florida led to uncovering the multiple, separate, secret lives of our dad.

Much of the information I gathered came from the memories of my two older sisters. The miracles came when we found proof of their memories.

In our travels and research, we crossed the Atlantic Ocean, the St. Johns River, the Tennessee River, the Ohio River, and the Tallapoosa River. We sat on the banks of the Tallapoosa River and listened to the roar of the water as it flowed through the Southland of Georgia. We walked the streams of our ancestors' farmlands, took pictures of the old barn still standing there, and revisited the family graveyard on a hilltop surrounded by trees.

At times, traveling with my two sisters became my story. Because of their age, several years older than I, I had not bonded with them in our family life. Certainly their experiences growing up with Dad were totally different from my life with him.

This journey we were on, together, was emotional in a different way, for the three of us. Often one sister would cry; one would curse; one would laugh, all trying to deal with our dad's indiscretions.

I am sure I can never capture in words a description of this time with my sisters. Precious, cherished memories we share. Understanding of our dad's life became our common ground. Love for him and for each other became our only purpose.

By the end of our research, I knew the complete story of my dad's life.

Seems like there were always choices for me to make. I had made the choice to discover the truth of dad's life, now I had the choice of what to do with what I now knew. Write a book or not?

This was not my only question. Am I capable of writing a book? How do I get started?

After my morning walk along the shore of Charlotte Harbor, I found myself wandering around our condo area.

Friends encountered always had the question for me, "Writing that book yet?"

Day after day, my answer remained the same, "Not yet."

On a morning such as this, when I walked in the door, my phone was ringing. What a wonderful surprise to hear the voice of my dear friend Wayne. Wayne and his wife, Juanita, became our friends when I worked at Jacobson's store (1977-1983).

Now living in Alabama, Wayne never had a lot of time to visit, but he came once in a while and called, keeping in touch.

Frank and I admired Wayne and are proud to have him as our friend.

After the phone greetings, there it came, the same question, "Have you started writing your book?"

I spent the next fifteen minutes explaining to Wayne why I was not writing. The formidable obstacle, how do I get started?

Stern, yet caring, he chose his words carefully, "Martha, you are a great story teller, you are smart and disciplined. Take a pen and a piece of paper and write your story down just as you would tell it to me."

I remember uttering, "I'll try."

"You will do this," Wayne's parting words before he hung up the phone.

The next morning I woke up; made my usual cereal; sat on the screened porch for some time; washed my face; got dressed; poured myself another cup of coffee.

There would be no walking this morning. I took a TV tray to my small desk that sat in the corner of my bedroom; opened the tray; sat down on the desk stool; reached over, picking up one sheet of lined notebook paper and the ballpoint pen that lay next to the stack of paper on the tray; took the pen in my right hand and assumed the writing position.

Nothing happened! Gazing out the window; searching the puffy, white clouds as they rolled across the pale blue sky; my voice was pleading, "If I am to write this book, let me begin or let me put away all this research material that now lies in stacks all round my bedroom. I know the complete story of my dad's life. I have no need to share it with anyone; but, by telling his story if it will fill a need in someone else's life, then that is my purpose."

After a few minutes, I began to write. Page after page, the stack of unused notebook paper ran out and much more was needed.

As the hours, days, months went by; I was able to blend my organizational and creativity skills in placing my dad's life story in the 101 years of history.

Not knowing if my words would ever be published in a book, I kept pouring them onto the notebook paper. When the stack of written pages grew to hundreds, I called my niece, Brenda, for help.

Brenda is an excellent typist and I knew I could trust her. I had no doubts about the story I was writing, but still had no idea if this would ever be a book.

Brenda would be the first person to read my handwritten words. Eager to get the typing started, Brenda hurried off to her typing room. I waited in her living room.

Click, click, click, click; the humming of the typewriter resonated throughout the house. After some time had gone by, there was silence. Thinking Brenda was taking a break, I went in to join her.

There sat Brenda with her feet propped up, manuscript in her hand enjoying the read.

"Well?" I questioned.

"Oh, Aunt Martha, it is good!" Brenda explained, "I had to see what was going to happen. I couldn't wait to get to it with my typing."

"Well?" I repeated myself, "Do we have the beginnings of a book?"

"Not only a book, Aunt Martha, but a very good book." Brenda's words were honest. From that time on there would be many hours writing for me, typing for her and countless conversations. She was my sounding board, always encouraging when I was tired, questioning my ability and just wanting to get to "the end."

At one point I was complaining so much to Brenda, she said to me, "Aunt Martha, you have him on a train. You can have the train wreck and it's all over!"

I wondered if my niece, Brenda, had been talking to my editor friend, Sheila. It seemed as though they both had a way to motivate me into moving forward. With their motivation, I was not going to be a quitter.

Underlining the words I wrote in the third chapter of the manuscript: CROSSING IN THE RAIN; this became the title of my book. From the beginning until the end, my life was filled with mystical events and vivid dreams. Often I wasn't sure if I or someone else was doing the writing.

Sitting on my porch in Pine Island, my publisher said, "I am not one to believe in things I can't see or hear. I fought in the fields of Vietnam so I am not afraid of things unknown. While reading **Crossing in the Rain** several unexplained things happened to me; not that made me afraid, but that made me realize there is a reason this story should be told.

"Martha, it doesn't matter if I publish this book. It is a book that needs to be published."

Finally, in 1996, I held my book, **Crossing in the Rain,** in my hands.

Chapter 37

The Right Decision

Libraries, genealogy groups, book stores and different organizations called; filling my calendar with speaking engagements and book signings.

The questions poured in, ranged from; how did you get started writing, to how did you get published, and what about marketing? The most asked question – how did you do all the research?

My answers always started the same way, "It's not easy. I had no one to teach me how to do any of these things. I researched the process as well as the story, learning each step as I came to it. With my knowledge and what I call 'my God-given talent' I have been successful."

When the question comes up, why did you write this story? I describe a discussion I encountered during one of my book signings in an art gallery on Pine Island.

An older gentleman came up to me and asked if I had a moment where he could speak to me in private.

Walking across the street, we stood on the shore of Charlotte Harbor. Gazing out across the water, the man hesitated, and then began, "After reading your book, ***Crossing in the Rain***, I decided to try to find my real family. I knew I was adopted as a baby. I also knew the name of the adoption agency in Chicago. I called the agency inquiring about my adoption records. Who were my real parents?

"With little faith that I would ever get this question answered, I was surprised when several days later the agency called me.

"We have found your biological mother and she has agreed to meet you if that is what you want! We are giving you her phone number and address with her permission."

Even now, telling me his story, the man became very nervous.

"It's okay," I assured him. "I understand."

With encouragement, he continued, "The address was in a town only fifty miles from my home. I picked up the phone and dialed. A sweet voice answered, an agreement was made, and I would drive to her house the next day.

"I rang the door bell, the door opened; there stood my mother."

Tears ran down his face and also mine as I let him gather his thoughts to continue telling me about his mother.

"She is now in her nineties, but she was just a young girl when she got pregnant out of wedlock. Unable to keep her baby, she chose adoption.

"Later she did marry, but she never had any more children. Her husband passed away and she was left alone.

"She recalled the day, the adoption agency called asking if she would be willing to meet her son. She had been wondering why she was living to be so old. Now she knew; to meet her son.

"My adopted parents had been wonderful to me and gave me a good life. They have now passed away. I was like my mother, left alone."

He took my hands, holding them caringly, "Mrs. Perritti, because of you, I now know my mother and she has me in her life. Reading your words in your book gave me the courage to seek out and find my mother. We both thank you for sharing your story."

As the man and I walked back to the art gallery, it was I who now thanked him for sharing his story with me.

If there were ever to be a reason why I wrote **Crossing in the Rain,** I now knew the why and know I made the right decision to publish my father's true story.

Chapter 38

Changes – Personal and Historical

Anger and harassment were directed toward me by several of my brothers and sisters. Jealousy uncoiled its ugly head as they began to blame me for my relationship with my dad and now with my husband and my son. I believe the phrase used was, "Spoiled and always been spoiled!"

My publishing personal beliefs about the story of my dad's life opened the window for their criticism. The three sisters, who did all the research with me and I never wavered from our beliefs in the truth of my story.

The change in my life paled in comparison to the lives of immigrants coming ashore on American soil.

1991 – Immigration into America

Words of Time Magazine's Robert Hughes, "a construction of mind, not of race or inherited class or ancestral territory ... America is a collective act of imagination that's making never ends."

Just as the immigrants were looking for change in their lives, the citizens of America would need to change as well.

1993 – The Web

This is the phenomenon that brought about the greatest change in our history. After computers were invented, the Internet was a globe-circling network of supercomputers run by experts at major institutions. In 1990, the World Wide Web system was available to the super computers only.

Then, in 1993, software was released that put the Web within reach of every computer. Millions of ordinary people started surfing the Web. From weather reports to shopping, they were all available with a click of the mouse.

Change takes charge – William (Bill) Clinton, United States President 1993-2001. The torch was passed to this 46-year old, born after World War II. His generation, sometimes called baby boomers, had to change their ideas of having the older generation running things, suddenly there's a guy their age who is president of the United States.

Bill Clinton graduated from Georgetown University in 1968; attended Oxford University in England as a Rhodes Scholar; graduated from Yale School Law, 1973.

From President Bill Clinton's Inaugural address:

"There is nothing wrong with America that cannot be cured by what is right with America. ...To renew America, we ... must do what no generation has had to do before."

Ideas of Heaven change because of the Hubble Telescope. 1609, Galileo first pointed a telescope at the heavens. 1993, The United States using a bus-size satellite crammed with cameras, communications gear, and a main mirror nearly eight feet in diameter; embarked on a mission to gauge the age of the universe.

Till this day, the Hubble is sending spectacular images of never-before-seen stars and galaxies.

1997 –

As the United States trail blazes Mars, other planets and stars, I find myself very confident with my changing world.

Chapter 39

What About Mother?

Speaking to groups and individuals who read my book **Crossing in the Rain**, I was often asked, "How much of your dad's story did your mother know?"

With admiration people would say, "What a wonderful woman. What gave her that spirit of steadfastness and endurance?"

Facing the reality that I knew very little about my mother, I began to dwell on what made her the way she was.

Taken away from the Tennessee Valley when I was four years old, I returned only on brief visits with relatives. Seldom did Mother speak of life in the valley. With hesitation she did tell me about the day I was born. I have no memories of Grandma's farmhouse in the valley. When I asked about Grandma Lucinda, Mother would tell me only that she died when I was a baby. Her last words "Take care of my little Martha Lou."

Mother never spoke of her heritage. Beyond the fertile valley of the Tennessee River, I had no idea where she came from.

Just as I had done when I made a phone call to my older sister seeking knowledge of my dad's life, I now picked up the phone, asking to speak to a cousin that lives in the valley.

The conversation was brief: "Nila, do you know anything about our mother's heritage?" Her mother and my mother were sisters.

"Martha Lou," she said, "If you will come to my house I will tell you about your heritage."

The door now opened, I stepped into the past. Revelations of my people and my discoveries were sometimes unbearable.

I was sixty years old when I learned that my great-great-great-grandma Polly; my great-great grandma Martha and great-grandma Rhoda were Native American, Cherokee Indians.

For three years, their lives became my life. Gazing from the mountaintops of the Cumberland Gap, I imagined their life in the valleys; standing in the forgotten fort of Fort Payne, I cried for the pain and sorrow of the Trail of Tears; walking the trails in the forest of the Warrior Mountains, I found my heritage.

No questions were necessary as to why my mother never told me about these Cherokee women. Understanding the history, I understood the protection of a mother.

Once again, I had gathered all the research; I knew my story; the writer in me was anxious.

I had answered one of the questions about my mother. The other question, how much did she know about my dad, still remains a mystery.

The answer to what gave my mother her endurance to maintain her dignity, faith and courage - the answer is her heritage. Engrained with the spirit of Great, Great, Great-Grandma Polly, Great, Great-Grandma Martha and Great-Grandma Rhoda, her life became an example of theirs.

Mother often told me that early in the morning or late afternoon, she would see her mother walk down to the pond a short distance in back of the house. Grandma Lucinda would kneel there in a praying position. No one knew if words were spoken or the subject of her meditation.

Today, many, many years later as I stand in my praying spot, I do believe that Grandma Lucinda's thoughts and mine are exactly the same.

"Thank you for all that I have and all that I am."

Velvie Killgore – Martha Lou's Mother
She was mother to 10 children.

The Pine Island Eagle

Wednesday,
January 28, 2004

Volume 27 No. 18

PRSRT STD
U.S. Postage
PAID
Permit No. 521
Fort Myers, FL

Free

Serving Matlacha, Pine Island Center, Pineland, Bokeelia and St. James City

THE PINE ISLAND EAGLE   JANUARY 28, 2004, PAGE 17

Standing Against the Wind arrives at Pine Island Library

Standing against the Wind (Lifestyles Press), an epic tale of the Cherokee Nation, is narrated through three of Perritti's great grandmothers. Their story exemplifies the plight of thousands of Native Americans through five generations of the author's family. The novel has been surpassed in part, to Gold Mountain by reviewers. Recently it was selected to show at the London Book Fair. The cover on the book has an actual image of Perritti's great grandmother in the background.

For readers who enjoy history, this book should be on the "to read" list. It reveals the richness of the Cherokee culture in a lone-time, that covers the Indian removal program, the Trail of Tears and the Civil War up through the early 1900s. The first edition is available on the internet on Amazon.com, at Books and More in Matlacha, at Crossed Palm Gallery in Bokeelia, on Sanibel at The Island Book Nook, MacIntosh Book Shop, Inc. and the Sanibel Island Book Shop. In Fort Myers, it is available at the Heritage Bookstore.

Perritti to appear at Lee County's Celebration of Authors, Art on Jan. 23

Martha Perritti, local author and resident of Pine Island, will appear at Celebration of Authors and Art 2004, sponsored by the Friends Foundation for the Lee County Library

Pine Island resident and author, Martha Lou Perritti "shelves" her new historical novel, Standing against the Wind at the Pine Island Library. It joins her other books: Crossing in the Rain and her cook books.

System. The event will take place on January 23 in the Historic Collier Arcade, 1520 Broadway, Fort Myers. Hours: Open from 4 to 8 p.m. It's free and the public. Showcasing for-used novel, Standing

against the Wind, along with her first novel, Crossing in the Rain and two of her cook books, Perritti will sign books and meet event attendees at her book display. Perritti will also answer questions about her latest novel, Standing against the Wind. Based on her family's history, the story is about three of her great grandmothers—all full-blooded Cherokee women. One experienced the Trail of Tears, one the lemon of the Civil War and the other was forced from her home and land.

Standing against the Wind will educate most readers on the richness of the Cherokee culture—as well as inform them of the tragic reverberations of the Indian Removal Program.

The novel is available on Amazon.com and at Perritti's favorite local stores in the Pine Island area: Books & More in Matlacha and Crossed Palms Gallery in Bokeelia.

For speaking engagements or interviews with Perritti, contact Lynda Long at email (preferred method): LKL47@comcast.net, or call 239/282-1331. For more information about Celebration of Authors and Art 2004, call 239-542-0363.

Chapter 40

"Standing Against the Wind"

Now that I had a family history book and a cookbook published, I no longer doubted my ability to write a book.

Repeating the process, I published a new cookbook *"Martha Lou's Kitchen."* I began the arduous task of writing the history of the Cherokee Nation with the story of my three grandmothers contained within.

Criticism of a few family members was not going to stop me from writing. Encouragement and support from others was welcomed, but when the pen and paper came together I was alone.

As the days passed and the pages of notebook paper filled with words, I often walked the shore of Charlotte Harbor. Watching the seagulls in their quest across the water, I was amazed at how often they struggled, flying against the wind.

Strong and never falling, the seagull prevailed. The wind blew across my face; I stood with memories of all I knew about the Cherokee and felt the presence of three women.

How strong the understanding of previous generations. How grand these women were as they were STANDING AGAINST THE WIND.

In 2003, *"Standing Against the Wind"* was published. Interest in my historical novel created the necessity of a publicist.

Lynda had been a dear friend, now she was my publicist. With her expertise I have been successful in marketing my written works.

Pine Island, here I am, the young girl from the valley, all grown up, sixty four years old, in fact.

A military wife, a mother and an accomplished author, was I now at the end of the road?

Not if my husband and my son had anything to say about it. No, we were headed for a new life once again.

While Frank had been boating, fishing, playing tennis and I had been writing, our son was building a career that led him to Tallahassee, the capital city of Florida.

Graduating from Florida State University with a masters degree, he not only became an avid fan of the Florida State Seminoles; he became a respected member of the administrative staff of the State of Florida.

Great, Great Grandfather William Henderson's
Grave site, Mobile, Alabama

Great, Great Grandfather William Henderson's
grave site in Mobile, Alabama

Martha Lou and Frank Perritti – Golden Eagle Country Club
Tallahassee, Florida - 2005

Chapter 41

Pine Island – Not the End of the Road

"Martha, have you ever lived in a place you didn't 'just love'?" Someone once asked me this question.

"No," was my quick reply. Reason being, of all the places I have lived, I left with only the best of memories.

Place is in the heart, not this land or that. Moving to Pine Island, Frank and I had chosen the absolute perfect place on earth to live out the rest of our lives. Our island in the sun; the days long and lazy; we were blessed with a good life, meant to last forever.

The saying is, everything happens for a reason. In our case, Frank, Richard and I, it seems everything happens for a challenge.

As Richard settled into his life in Tallahassee, the more Frank and I wanted to be a part of his life there. He had little time to travel and visit us in Pine Island.

The motivation to move in order to be near our son won out over deciding to continue living on Pine Island.

True, our life style would change drastically, but our life as a family had been all about changes and, I had become an author/lecturer.

Leaving Pine Island was not easy. No doubt my life had always been affected by the place I called home at the time. Tears were shed and left in the winds of Charlotte Harbor.

In my deepest thoughts my real home is my birthplace, the weather-board farmhouse, in the middle of a cotton field, in the valley of the Tennessee River of North Alabama.

No matter how far I travel or what I become, I will forever be from this fertile valley.

Should you look for me in Tallahassee, I will probably be the lady bending down to pick up a lost penny!

Martha Lou with students at an Indian Festival
Lawrence City, Alabama

Martha Lou – Punta Gorda Yacht Club
Lecture and Book Signing

Lecturing at the Punta Gorda Yacht Club

Signing books at the Punta Gorda Yacht Club

Martha Lou at her book signing
Punta Gorda Yacht Club

From the Author

Creation of life – many life stories have been written, mine is just one of millions.

Often I feel alone as I take my stand, a free woman in a free country. The question being, do I stand alone? I have only to look within myself to believe there are different Marthas all living in one body and generations of women in our world just like me.

Writing this book, I have explored how I became the person I am. It's the story of how I got here from there; the history of my family that lived in a fertile valley; the story of my ancestors who paved my way to becoming an author, a military wife and a mother.

When my cousin Donna calls, my husband jokes with her when she asked to speak to me. He tells her I am washing his car or mowing the lawn. Her reply to this, "No, that is your dream Martha, not the Martha I know."

Actually, Donna, you do know the dream Martha; the young girl from the valley who dreamed of a good life; a daughter to be proud of; a committed wife and mother and a writer.

Standing in the Research Center of the Smithsonian Museum, The National Museum of American Indian in Washington, DC, September 8, 2006, was the dream come true Martha.

I did not stand alone on that day as I talked about and presented my book **"*Standing Against the Wind.*"** My written story of my ancestors captured the spirit of a nation never to be forgotten.

No doubt, I embody the strength and courage of my Cherokee heritage. Just as the generations before me endured their challenges, my goal is to live as an example of their character.

One thing is certain, as long as I have a mind and a matter, I will write.

Message from Martha

-Military Wife-

The face of our nation is seen in the faces of our military wives. Yesterday, today and tomorrow their challenges are often insurmountable. The military paycheck is no compensation for the sacrifice of one's life.

When our nation is at war, these sacrifices multiply. Our nation is, at this time, at war with terrorism; within our borders and abroad. Every citizen of every community in America needs to focus on the security of our nation.

The military men and women and their families hold the key to our protection. Our nation must remain vigilant in our support of our military forces.

To all military wives, let me express to you from my experience, "You do not stand alone."

You have been given the opportunity to touch people's lives all around the world; experiences of travel, meeting people of all races; and, most of all, the unending friendships and bonding with other military families.

In the words of my dear friend Harriette, when I asked her how I could pay her for taking such good care of my son when I was sick, "You pass the legacy of commitment of the military wife by giving it to others."

To past, present and future military wives, I salute you for your courage and spirit.

Most important – when retirement time comes – don't be afraid – just as for me, another distant dream beckons you.

List of References

The Young People's Encyclopedia of the United States,
        General Editor: William E. Shapiro, The Millbrook
        Press, Inc., 1992

Events that Shaped the Century by the Editors of Time-Life
        Books, Alexandria, Virginia

Website: www.MarthaLouPerritti.com

Website: www.globalsecuirty.org

Website: http://en.widipedia.org

Website: http://www.cv18.com/history.html

Website: http://www.epodunk.com

Website: www.MOAA.org